FREE WITHIN OURSELVES

OURSELVES

The Harlem Renaissance

AFRICAN-AMERICAN EXPERIENCE

FREE WITHIN
OURSELVES

The Harlem Renaissance

by Geoffrey Jacques

FRANKLIN WATTS   *A Division of Grolier Publishing*
New York/London/Hong Kong/Sydney/Danbury, Connecticut

Harlem, 1920

Photo credits ©: AP/Wide World Photos: 52, 55, 71; Archive Photos: 47 (Frank Driggs Collection), 48; Bettmann Archive: 97 (John Springer Collection); Brown Brothers: 4; Countee Cullen Papers, Amistad Research Center: 29; Harmon Foundation Collection: 16; Library of Congress: 11, 35 (Griff Davis); New York Public Library Picture Collection: 76, 79, 82, 84, 87, 94; New York Public Library, Schomburg Center for Research in Black Culture: 24, 26; Prints and Photographs Collection, Moorland-Spingarn Research Center, Howard University: 39; UPI/Bettmann: 18, 45, 61, 63, 65, 81; William Loren Katz: 89.

Library of Congress Cataloging-in-Publication Data

Jacques, Geoffrey.
  Free within ourselves: the Harlem Renaissance / by Geoffrey Jacques.
    p.   cm. — (African-American experience)
  Includes bibliographical references (pp. 111–118) and index.
  Summary: Discusses the rise of the Harlem Renaissance in the early twentieth century and the artists responsible for the art, music, theater, prose, and poetry created in that era.
  ISBN 0-531-11272-1
    1. Harlem Renaissance—Juvenile literature. 2. Afro-American arts—Juvenile literature. [1. Harlem Renaissance. 2. Afro-American arts.] I. Title. II. Series.
NX512.3.A35J23   1996
700′.89′9607307471—dc20   96-24340
                                                            CIP
                                                             AC

TABLE OF CONTENTS

ONE

Old and New Negroes

In the beginning of the twentieth century, a political and cultural conflict arose in the African-American community that would shape African-American art, literature, thought, and politics for years to come. The conflict concerned the differing strategies black Americans should adopt for coping with, surviving, and overcoming the racism that pervaded American society.

BOOKER T. WASHINGTON AND W. E. B. DU BOIS

On one side stood Booker T. Washington whose strategy emerged from the ruins of a defeated Reconstruction. Blacks in the South had found themselves enmeshed in a seamless web of oppression. As a response to this oppression, Booker T. Washington counseled blacks to accommodate themselves to the victorious southern white segregated order. In his autobiography published in 1901, *Up From Slavery*, he stated that his goal at Tuskegee, the school he founded, was to give students an industrial education, "such a practical knowledge of some one industry...that they would be sure of knowing how to make a living." His students would be taught "to study actual things instead of mere books alone."[1] Washington abandoned agitation for political and socal equality, favoring instead educational uplift and economic advancement.

Two years later, in 1903, W. E. B. Du Bois posed an opposite strategy in *The Souls of Black Folk*—that black people must challenge racism everywhere. Soon after, Du Bois joined with other reformers to found the NAACP. *The Souls of Black Folk* became the first document of the "New Negro," who took pride in the race and affirmed the self. Those who subscribed to Booker T. Washington's views were regarded as "Old Negroes"; those who sided with Du Bois were "New Negroes." The Harlem Renaissance was a celebration of the "New Negro" but it also was born in the intellectual ferment that flowed from the concept of a "New Negro."

JACK JOHNSON

At the same time a young African-American man from Galveston, Texas, was getting ready to challenge white supremacy in an unexpected way. He was training to become the heavyweight boxing champion of the world. Jack Johnson became the embodiment of the "New Negro" when on July 4, 1910, in Reno, Nevada, after years of effort he defeated the "Great White Hope," James Jeffries. Johnson was the first black heavyweight champion of the world. Johnson has said that when he was in the ring with Jeffries, he was not only fighting his opponent but the entire throng of spectators who hurled racial epithets at the black boxer. Johnson's victory brought jubilation to the black masses—and some terror too as more than one African-American was set upon by mobs of angry whites.

Johnson retired from the ring a celebrity. An amateur cellist, he played in cabarets and nightclubs, and eventually operated a Harlem nightspot, the Club Deluxe. After a few years, Johnson entered into a business arrangement with a bootlegger named Owney Madden who took over the club and renamed it. And so Johnson enters the history of the Harlem Renaissance, not only as the prototypical "New Negro" due to his world championship, but as a partner in the nightclub that brought Duke Ellington to fame, the Cotton Club.

MARCUS GARVEY, BLACK NATIONALIST

Another contribution to the philosophical conflict of the Old and New Negroes that was to affect the Harlem Renaissance came from the orator and leader Marcus Garvey. On August 2, 1920, 25,000 African-Americans, possibly the largest political gathering of black people in the history of North America, attended a speech by Marcus Garvey at Madison Square Garden in New York City. A native of Jamaica who moved to Harlem in 1916, Garvey founded the United Negro Improvement Association (U.N.I.A.) and a weekly newspaper, *Negro World.* By the time of his 1920 speech, Garvey was probably the most famous man in the world among black people.

"We shall now organize the 400 million Negroes of the world into a vast organization to plant the banner of freedom on the great continent of Africa," Garvey told his Madison Square Garden audience.

"If Europe is for Europeans, then Africa shall be for the black peoples of the world. We say it; we mean it." It was the first time such an explicit African nationalist message had been announced so publicly. "It is time," Garvey said, "for the 400 million Negroes to claim Africa for themselves."[2]

It was a stirring message, and for a time Garvey's movement animated Harlem and the African world. The black nationalist preached racial segragation. Garvey was the first to convince millions of people of African descent to be proud of their heritage: of Africa, its greatness, and their own dark skin and kinky hair. Garvey's U.N.I.A. made it possible for the Harlem Renaissance to be more than just a protest movement. His celebration of African people was echoed by the writers and artists of the Renaissance.

PAUL LAURENCE DUNBAR

In literature the forerunner of the renaissance writers was Paul Laurence Dunbar (1872–1906), at the turn of the century, the country's best known African-American poet and novelist. Though born in Dayton, Ohio, much of Dunbar's verse and fiction echoed the life and language of the African-American South. *Lyrics of the Lowly Life,* Dunbar's most famous book, has poems written in both standard English and African-American English.

Much of Dunbar's poetry has home and family as its main theme. But he is often sharp and poignant in addressing questions related to racism. Like many great artists, Dunbar sought to address race questions not simply from a narrow, provincial point of view. He found a wider context by writing more abstractly of freedom. The poem "Sympathy," for

Paul Laurence Dunbar

example, with its metaphor of the caged bird, which poet Maya Angelou would use many years later as the title of her best-selling memoir, is an example of universalizing racial issues:

I know what the caged bird feels, alas!
When the sun is bright on the upland slopes
When the wind stirs soft through the springing grass
And the river flows like a stream of glass;
When the first bird sings and the first bud opes,
And the faint perfume from its chalice steals—
I know what the caged bird feels!

I know why he beats his wing!

It is not a carol of joy or glee,
But a prayer that he sends from his heart's deep core,
But a plea, that upward to Heaven he flings—
I know why the caged bird sings![3]

The reader may or may not know the specific reference made by the poet, but the pathos suggested by the title and weaved throughout the poem, the immediate identification the reader has with the caged bird, and the haunting, beautiful lyricism all create the conclusion that what goes for the bird might go for the human spirit, bound and yearning for freedom.

This universalist concept is also alive in Dunbar's most famous poem, "We Wear the Mask":

12

We wear the mask that grins and lies,
It hides our cheeks and shades our eyes,
This debt we pay to human guile;
With torn and bleeding hearts we smile,
And mouth with myriad subtleties.[4]

For a century now, this poem has served as an artistic expression of that "double consciousness" that Du Bois wrote of so eloquently in *The Souls of Black Folk*.

Though he continued to write in stylized southern Negro dialect to meet the intense demands of his white audiences, Dunbar never favored this aspect of his talent. Yet his facility with this style would help mark him as a master of twentieth century poetry. African-American poets who wrote in dialect have, for nearly a century, followed in the steps of Dunbar, one of the early masters of verse based on American (as opposed to British-inflected) speech. In all, he published six books of verse. *Lyrics of the Lowly Life* was issued by a major publishing house, Dodd, Mead and Company, that earlier had published Dunbar's *Majors and Minors*.

In his 1902 novel, *The Sport of the Gods*, Dunbar treats with sympathy southern African-Americans who have just migrated north. In New York these immigrants find a life altogether different from the one they left. Dunbar depicts a black New York of gambling, drinking, and loose morals. It is a turbulent, unsettled world where the inhabitants are caught between two cultures: on the one hand that of the hardworking, striving southern emigrant; on the other, that of the sportsman, the gambler, the musician, the actor. At the same time, it is a city of freedom, where legalized racial segregation doesn't exist, and where the rule of law means not only that justice is possible, but that some whites might even come to the defense of a black person unjustly accused of crime.

Dunbar also shows New York's "Black Bohemia," the center of the city's growing black theatrical world. The saloons in this area of Manhattan—roughly between Twenty-fourth and Fortieth streets and Fifth and Seventh avenues—were home to writers, actors, musicians, singers, prizefighters, and others. People like W. E. B. Du Bois and James Weldon Johnson frequented these establishments, where musicians like pianist-composer Eubie Blake often played. Here many New Yorkers first heard the new music called ragtime.

Although there were other accomplished African-American writers in the nineteenth century, Paul Laurence Dunbar was the first major black literary artist. His work influenced the Harlem Renaissance.

The Harlem Renaissance owes its success to those who nurtured the movement, many of whom were artists in their own right. Among them were: Jessie Fauset, novelist and literary editor of the NAACP magazine, the *Crisis*; Charles Johnson, editor of *Opportunity*, the magazine of the Urban League; Alain Locke, who edited the Harlem Renaissance anthology, *The New Negro*; William Stanley Braithwaite, anthologist and poetry editor for the *Boston Evening Transcript*; James Weldon Johnson, a poet, anthologist, and NAACP leader; and W. E. B. Du Bois, editor of the *Crisis*, novelist, essayist, historian, and political leader.

Two of the most important African-American organizations, the National Association for the

Advancement of Colored People and the National Urban League, were founded in 1909 and in 1910 in New York. Both organizations were to play crucial roles in the Harlem Renaissance. Du Bois had moved to New York in 1910 to work as NAACP director of publicity and research and had started the *Crisis* magazine in November 1910. It was a radical magazine for its time, advocating woman's suffrage and the end of racial discrimination. The *Crisis* was destined to play an important role in the Harlem Renaissance, in part because its literary editor during the early 1920s was the novelist Jessie Fauset, and in part because its main editor was a poet and novelist as well as a scholar and political propagandist.

Du Bois' first novel, *The Quest of the Silver Fleece*, was published in 1911. William Stanley Braithwaite praised it when it first appeared. Braithwaite in his survey of blacks in American literature that was included in the Harlem Renaissance anthology, *The New Negro* (1925), commented that when the great epic novel of the south was written, *The Quest of the Silver Fleece* would prove to have been its forerunner.

Alain Locke is considered one of the chief interpreters of the Harlem Renaissance. He was a reviewer for the magazines *Opportunity* and *Phylon* and for many years taught philosophy at Howard University. His works include *Four Negro Poets* (1927); *Frederick Douglas, a Biography of Anti-Slavery* (1935); *Negro Art—Past and Present* (1936); and *The Negro and His Music* (1936).

JAMES WELDON JOHNSON

Johnson was an extraordinary, versatile promoter of the Harlem Renaissance who was also a poet of the Renaissance. Born in Jacksonville, Florida, he taught

Alain Locke

school and helped start the first African-American
daily newspaper there and became the first black
person to pass the Florida bar. With his brother,
J. Rosamond Johnson, he composed songs and shows

for the concert and Broadway stage. Many of their songs were hits, and with musician and composer Bob Cole, the Cole and Johnson Brothers were among the pioneers of modern American musical theater. The Johnson brothers wrote in 1900, "Lift Every Voice and Sing," which soon became known as the Negro national anthem. It is sung to this day. Johnson was a founding member of the American Society of Composers, Authors and Publishers (ASCAP), the largest songwriters organization in the world.

James Weldon Johnson was also a literary artist. His novel, *The Autobiography of an Ex-Coloured Man*, published in 1912, is considered a prototype of the modern African-American novel and a direct ancestor of books like Ralph Ellison's *Invisible Man.* Johnson's poem, "Fifty Years," commemorated the fiftieth anniversary of the Emancipation Proclamation. It was one of the first literary expressions of the New Negro that was to emerge in full force after World War I. At a time when black life seemed cheap in the face of lynchings, antiblack mob violence, and public massacres, Johnson's poem reminded it's readers that the wealth of the country was built largely by black labor. It called on African-Americans to claim the United States as their birthright and spoke of blood shed by abolitionists, soldiers, and a president in the cause of ending slavery. In contrast with the cool, light irony practiced by Johnson's friend and teacher Paul Laurence Dunbar, "Fifty Years" is a poem full of the fire of resistance.

In 1916, Johnson was appointed field secretary for the NAACP and led the organization's growth in the south. When he began, there were seventy-one NAACP branches, only three in the South. Three years later, there were three hundred and ten branches in

James Weldon Johnson

the NAACP, one hundred and thirty-one of them in the South.

Johnson also served for seven years in the U.S. diplomatic corps, with posts in Venezuela and Nicaragua. (For his poetry of the Harlem Renaissance, see Chapter 2.)

18

THE SURVEY GRAPHIC

In March 1924, Charles S. Johnson, the new editor of the National Urban League's monthly publication, *Opportunity*, hosted a dinner for Harlem literary artists to celebrate the publication of Jessie Fauset's first novel, *There Is Confusion.* The dinner was held at the Civic Club in Greenwich Village, the only upper-crust New York club without color or sex restrictions, where Afro-American intellectuals and prominent white liberals gathered.

Guests from the mainstream (white) literary world included playwrights Eugene O'Neill and Ridgely Torrence, editor H. L. Mencken, poet Carl Van Doren, publisher Horace Liveright, NAACP cofounder Oswald Garrison Villard, and art collector Albert Barnes. At the dinner, the downtown literary establishment met black writers including fiction writers Eric Walrond (who served for a time as an editor of Marcus Garvey's *Negro World* newspaper), Jessie Fauset, and Gwendolyn Bennett, and poets Georgia Douglas Johnson, Countee Cullen, and Langston Hughes. Howard philosophy professor and first African-American Rhodes Scholar Alain Locke was there, as was W. E. B. Du Bois and James Weldon Johnson.

Out of that dinner came an offer from Paul Kellogg, the editor of the magazine *Survey Graphic*, to devote a special issue to the artistic ferment in Harlem. The *Survey Graphic* for March 1925 was a special entitled "Harlem: Mecca of the New Negro." It was edited by Alain Locke and read by 42,000 people, double the magazine's regular circulation. The magazine was edited by Locke into book form and published at the end of the year. The anthology has an introduction by Locke, an essay on art by Albert Barnes, and William Stanley Braithwaite's survey, "The Negro in American Literature." Novelists Rudolph Fisher, Jean Toomer, and Zora Neale Hurston as well as John Matheus, Bruce Nugent, and Eric Walrond all contributed stories. Poets Countee Cullen, Claude McKay, James Weldon Johnson, Langston Hughes, Arna Bontemps, Georgia Douglas Johnson, Anne Spencer, and Angelina Grimke are all in the issue.

There are plays (including one by Jessie Fauset), folklore, and sociology, an essay on jazz by historian J. A. Rogers, and one on Harlem by James Weldon Johnson. And there are drawings by Aaron Douglas and Winold Reiss.

This was the first national publication for many of the younger authors. Langston Hughes wouldn't publish his first book until 1926, although Weldon Johnson and Toomer had already made their mark in the literary world.

By the time *The New Negro* reached bookstores in late 1925, the Harlem Renaissance was in full swing. The *Survey Graphic*'s special issue was an announcement that something new was happening in Harlem.

TWO

Harlem Verses

F*ifty Years And Other Poems* by James Weldon Johnson revealed a new mood in African-American literature. In 1921 nineteen-year-old Langston Hughes' poem, "The Negro Speaks of Rivers" appeared in the NAACP magazine, *Crisis*, and eighteen-year-old Countee Cullen's "I Have a Rendezvous with Life" was published in Manhattan's De Witt Clinton High School literary magazine. In 1922, James Weldon Johnson's anthology *The Book of American Negro Poetry* and Claude McKay's *Harlem Shadows* arrived on the literary scene. Along with Alain Locke's collection, *The New Negro* of 1925, they were the harbingers of the poetry of the Harlem Renaissance.

THE RED SUMMER OF 1919

After World War I, two hundred thousand African-American soldiers who had fought in the segregated United States Army returned home. After fighting for their country, many expected to be treated like other citizens. Thousands of blacks had migrated to the north to work in jobs that, not long before, had been reserved for white immigrants. In addition, labor unrest followed World War I as workers fought for better wages and working conditions in the expanding industries. Often strikes were waged by unions that barred black people from membership. Employers hired black workers as strikebreakers. Forced to choose between a job and solidarity with white workers who barred them from membership in the striking unions, blacks chose to work.

In that turbulent year, the United States was rocking with race and labor violence. A general strike in Seattle had many fearing the country was on the verge of revolution. That terrible summer, black people, for the first time since the end of Reconstruction, rose to fight the racist rioters. In Washington, Chicago, Tulsa, and elsewhere, black people defended themselves with arms. And for the first time in a half-century, black people weren't the only victims in antiblack riots. White racists died as well. In Chicago, where the worst riot of the year started after a white man killed a black teenager, five days of violence ended with eighteen blacks and fifteen whites dead, and over five hundred people of both races injured.

CLAUDE MCKAY

McKay was the poet of the Red Summer of 1919, voicing the anger and will to fight back that seized Afro-America's young generation. In the summer of 1919, McKay traveled around the country, working as a dining-car waiter on the Pennsylvania railroad, and saw the outbreak of antiblack violence.

"If We Must Die" is a defiant call to arms against the brutality heaped upon black people in scores of cities that summer:

22

If we must die, let it not be like hogs
Hunted and penned in an inglorious spot,
While round us bark the mad and hungry dogs,
Making their mock at our accursed lot.
If we must die, O let us nobly die,
Like men we'll face the murderous, cowardly pack,
Pressed to the wall, dying, but fighting back![1]

McKay was preeminently the poet of rebellion, according to James Weldon Johnson, expressing the feelings and reactions the Negro in America was experiencing. "If We Must Die" and "The Lynching" were published in 1919 in the socialist magazine *The Liberator,* of which McKay was associate editor. They were included in *Harlem Shadows* in 1922.

"If We Must Die" found a permanent place in English-language literature. Years later, during another war, the British Prime Minister Winston Churchill was heard on the radio, reading McKay's poem to a defiant and heroic British people as Adolph Hitler's bombs fell on London.

In 1916 Claude McKay had sent literary critic William Stanley Braithwaite some poems. McKay was working at the time as a waiter in a Hanover, New Hampshire, resort hotel and had no idea that Braithwaite was African-American. Braithwaite replied that any reader could tell the author was a Negro. Because of the almost insurmountable prejudice against all things Negro, Braithwaite advised him to send to magazines only poems that did not betray his racial identity. Ironically, the poems McKay was writing as he worked manual labor jobs throughout the northeast were some of the first poems of the New Negro of the 1920s.

William Stanley Braithwaite

Claude McKay wasn't only a poet of social protest. He also wrote beautiful lyrics of love and life. Frank Harris, the great Irish editor of *Pearson's* magazine, told the young poet he had a classical feeling and a modern way of expressing it. Of the ten books McKay published during his lifetime, four were poetry. The first two, *Songs of Jamaica* (1912) and *Constab Ballads* (1912), were published in his native

Jamaica. *Spring in New Hampshire* was issued in 1920. The publication of *Harlem Shadows* (1922) by a major U.S. publishing house, Harcourt, Brace & Company, marked, according to Arna Bontemps in *Harlem Renaissance Remembered*, the first time in nearly two decades that any such publisher had ventured to offer a book of poems by a living black poet.

COUNTEE CULLEN

Countee Cullen was an adopted child, raised by the Reverend Dr. Frederick A. Cullen and his wife Carolyn Belle. Doctor Cullen was pastor of Salem Methodist Episcopal Church in Harlem. After graduating De Witt Clinton High School, Countee Cullen went on to distinguish himself at New York University and Harvard.

The young poet showed his talent early for intensely lyrical poems. "I Have a Rendezvous with Life" (inspired by the famous World War I poem by Alan Seeger, "I Have a Rendevous with Death") was immediately popular. People began quoting Cullen's poem. Teachers read it to their classes. Ministers read it to fashionable congregations.

Many believed at this time that the two outstanding American lyric poets working in traditional forms were Edna St. Vincent Millay and Countee Cullen. Cullen admired Millay's poetry, which was the subject of his undergraduate thesis at New York University. Cullen wrote in traditional forms and meters, including rhymed iambic pentameter, the sonnet, and very occasionally, blank verse. He also wrote of love, truth, and beauty. Cullen's work has both the optimism and pessimism of youth. Intense race pride is evident in a poem such as "Heritage."

Countee Cullen

What is Africa to me:
Copper sun or scarlet sea,
Jungle star or jungle track,
Strong bronzed men, or regal black
Women from whose loins I sprang
When the birds of Eden sang?[2]

26

The black poets of the time treated opposition to racism as a universal theme. This is an example of Countee Cullen's, entitled "Incident":

Once riding in old Baltimore,
Heart-filled, head-filled with glee,
I saw a Baltimorean
Keep looking straight at me.

Now I was eight and very small,
And he was no whit bigger,
And so I smiled, but he poked out
His tongue, and called me, "Nigger."

I saw the whole of Baltimore
From May until December;
Of all the things that happened there
That's all that I remember.

Countee Cullen also wrote fiction and children's stories and worked as a teacher in the New York public schools.

LANGSTON HUGHES

Langston Hughes, born in 1902 in Joplin, Missouri, was raised mainly by his mother, Carrie Langston, who had literary and theatrical ambitions. His father, James Hughes, moved to Mexico soon after Langston was born. During a trip from Cleveland to Mexico to spend his high school graduation summer with his father—and to convince him to pay for college— Langston wrote "The Negro Speaks of Rivers," inspired as his train crossed the Mississippi River.

He published his first book, *The Weary Blues,*
in 1926. Hughes was the first to assimilate the
feeling of jazz and the blues in poetry through
his use of popular language. The title poem to
The Weary Blues captures the tone of twentieth
century American music:

Droning a drowsy syncopated tune,
Rocking back and forth to a mellow croon,
      I heard a Negro play.
Down on Lenox Avenue the other night
By the pale dull pallor of an old gas light
      He did a lazy sway
      He did a lazy sway
To the tune o' those Weary Blues.[3]

Like Walt Whitman, he uses simplicity and directness in
his attempt to create a folk poetry of the modern urban
African-American. Such an example is in "Epilogue":

I, too, sing America.

I am the darker brother.
They send me to eat in the kitchen
When company comes,
But I laugh,
And eat well,
And grow strong.

Tomorrow,
I'll sit at the table
When company comes.

The young Langston Hughes

Nobody'll dare
Say to me,
"Eat in the kitchen,"
Then.

Besides,
They'll see how beautiful I am
And be ashamed—

I, too, am America.

Hughes' method of composition was unusual. He was neither interested in telling a story in a conventional sense nor in self-expression. His poems, like many blues songs and folktales, were more like little morality tales.

Hughes documents small, almost infinitesimal slices of modern life. His poems resemble the newspaper photograph, which often serves as an illustration of an idea. Often, a Hughes poem will combine tales and songs he would pick up on the road.

He was one of the first American poets to make his living largely from giving readings, and he would walk the streets of African-American neighborhoods, picking up sayings, songs, and other material to use in his verses. Hughes would record verses from church services or songs overheard from stevedores on the streets of cities. In one trip to New Orleans, according to his biographer, Hughes picked up conjure lore. This included the sonorous names of remedies, potions, elixirs (Follow Me Powder, War and Confusion, Dust, Black Cat's Blood); rituals and recipes for life and death, sickness and health, love and revenge; even conjures to beat conjures. Much of this material eventually found its way into Hughes' poetry.

The poet's combination of aphorism and lyric, always suffused with a profound racial consciousness, delighted black audiences who found in his poems of race pride and social protest the everyday struggles they themselves were experiencing. That communication with his audience made Hughes one of the most popular poets of the century.

All day subdued, polite,
Kind, thoughtful to the faces that are white.
> *O, tribal dance!*
> *O, drums!*
> *O, veldt at night!*
Forgotten watch-fires on a hill somewhere!
> *O, songs that do not care!*

At six o'clock, or seven, or eight,
> *You're through.*
> *You've worked all day.*
> *Dark Harlem waits for you.*
> *The bus, the sub—*
> *Pay-nights a taxi*
> *Through the park.*

O, drums of life in Harlem after dark!
> *O, dreams!*
> *O, songs!*
> *O, saxophones at night!*
O, sweet relief from faces that are white!

("Negro Servant")

But concerns with "race" and racism did not make Hughes a narrow, provincial poet. His undeniably African-American-centered verse also has a universal aspect: the will to freedom and the struggle to realize identity. The fragility of the self faced with these dangers is one of his major themes.

LANGSTON HUGHES' POLITICAL POETRY

The leaders of intellectual and artistic Harlem paid little attention to politics. The most flamboyant political figure, Marcus Garvey, wasn't interested in practical politics. Most of the established leadership was still Republican, despite numerous betrayals of the black community by successive GOP presidents.

In 1928, NAACP secretary and novelist Walter White campaigned for Democratic presidential candidate Al Smith. But he was still a rarity among the African-American middle-class leadership. As for the radical politics, A. Philip Randolph, a socialist, embarked on his decades-long struggle to organize black Pullman Sleeping Car porters. The communists were a small political party in the 1920s, never attracting more than a handful of followers.

As the Depression deepened and there was little hope for the return of the prosperity of the 1920s, people began to fight evictions and unemployment. They joined left-wing organizations or more openly sympathized with them. In 1932, the communists nominated an African-American, James W. Ford, for vice president.

Langston Hughes developed left-wing sympathies. After trips to Cuba and Haiti in 1931, his poetry became increasingly dominated by social concerns. One poem lampooned the new Waldorf-Astoria hotel, urging the poor and homeless to impose themselves as guests in that monument to greed and avarice in the midst of seemingly universal poverty. Provoked by an advertisement for the new twenty-eight million dollar luxury hotel in the pages of *Vanity Fair*, "Advertisement for the Waldorf-Astoria" is a biting, ironic poem in the style of vernacular-poetry:

> *So when you've got no place else to go, homeless and hungry*
> *   ones, choose the Waldorf as a background for*
> *   your rags—*
> *(Or do you still consider the subway after midnight good*
> *   enough?)*

"Advertisement for the Waldorf-Astoria" deliberately avoids the lyricism of his 1920s poetry in favor of the speech-like rhythms of advertising copy. While academic critics dismissed "Advertisement for the Waldorf-Astoria" as mere propaganda, the poem is significant in the development of vernacular poetry.

In the spring of 1931, nine young African-American men in Scottsboro, Alabama, were convicted on trumped-up rape charges. Made an international political issue by the communist and left movement, the Scottsboro case is the first instance of southern racist justice being brought before the court of world public opinion. Though it took well over a decade for the last of the "Scottsboro Boys" to be set free, the publicity saved the young men's lives. The Scottsboro case was the first time since the end of Reconstruction that southern politics had become more than a regional issue.

Hughes visited the "Scottsboro Boys" in prison in Alabama and wrote in their honor, "Scottsboro" and "August 19." With its multiple voicing and conflicting narrators, "Scottsboro," though a piece of propaganda, is also a modernist poem. "August 19," with its simple yet haunting repetition of the date set for the execution of Scottsboro defendant Clarence Norris, achieves a rhetorical intensity reminiscent of some of Walt Whitman's poems:

In Alabama
A young black boy will die.
August 19th is the date.
Judges in high places
Still preserve their dignity
And dispose of cases.
August 19th is the date.
Rich people sit and fan
And sip cool drinks and do no work—
Yet they rule the land.
August 19th is the date.
The electric chair.
Swimmers on cool beaches
With their bodies bare.
August 19th is the date.

Hughes published poems in the left-wing literary journal *New Masses*, and became chairman of the League of Struggle for Negro Rights and a prominent member of the International Writers Congress. While some critics say his political activity had a negative effect on his poetry, and none would claim his 1930s work his best, it's easy enough to see how

Langston Hughes with students at an Atlanta, Georgia, school

the work he produced in those years led to the later triumphs of "Montage of a Dream Deferred" (1951) and "Ask Your Mama" (1961).

Hughes ranks with Walt Whitman as one of this country's most popular poets worldwide. He has been translated into nearly every major language; poets around the world revere him as an authentic poetic voice of the downtrodden and oppressed. He is considered one of the forerunners of the Negritude movement among African and Caribbean writers, and at one time in his career he was among the best-known American poets in the world.

JAMES WELDON JOHNSON

One of the most universally praised books by a Harlem poet in the 1920s was James Weldon Johnson's *God's Trombones: Seven Negro Sermons in Verse.* These seven poems tried to capture the cadence, spirit, and imagery of early southern black preachers.

The best of these poems is "The Creation," Johnson's vivid reworking of the bible story in the rhythm of southern African-American speech:

And God stepped out in space,
And he looked around and said:
I'm lonely—
I'll make me a world.

And as far as the eye of God could see
Darkness covered everything,
Blacker than a hundred midnights
Down in a cypress swamp.

Then God smiled,
And the light broke,
And the darkness rolled up on one side,
And the light stood shining on the other,
And God said: That's good![4]

Johnson recreated peoples' speech through paying close attention to actual speech patterns. In 1922, Johnson, in the first edition of his *The Book of*

American Negro Poetry, mounted a long critique of Negro-dialect poetry. In the preface to the second edition he modifies his critique by adding that poets like Langston Hughes and Sterling A. Brown do use a dialect; but it is not the dialect of the comic minstrel tradition or of the sentimental plantation tradition; it is the common, racy, living, authentic speech of the Negro in certain phases of real life.

STERLING A. BROWN

The end of the Harlem Renaissance marked for some writers who served apprenticeships there the beginning of their mature careers.

Although Sterling A. Brown (1901–89) never lived in Harlem, he published in the Urban League's magazine *Opportunity* in 1927, and is included in Countee Cullen's anthology, *Caroling Dusk* (1927). These first poems made quite an impression and led to his inclusion by James Weldon Johnson in the second edition of *The Book of American Negro Poetry* (1930).

The poems Brown published in the late 1920s would become the basis of his first collection, *Southern Road* (1932). With that book, Brown rose to the front ranks of African-American poets. Alain Locke called it a new era in Negro poetry. The book was praised by leading critics, from *The New York Times* to anthologist Louis Untermeyer.

Two things distinguished Brown from his predecessors. The first was summed up by Johnson in his preface to *The Book of Negro Poetry*. Brown writes a form of dialect poetry, but it is different from traditional dialect poetry, which Johnson described as "an instrument with but two full stops, humor and pathos." Brown writes in a form of dialect that has nothing to do with the traditional, minstrel-influenced dialect of previous African-American poets. Brown's dialect is the common, racy, living authentic speech of the Negro.

The second distinguishing characteristic of Brown's verse is that, unlike Hughes or any of the other Harlem poets, Brown saw himself as the poetic voice of the rural southern African-American. In his poems, sharecroppers and other black southerners tell tales of everyday life. Brown wrote few personal lyrics. His most powerful poems, such as his tribute to blues singer Gertrude "Ma" Rainey, are written in the voices of others. Brown's ear for the rhythms of everyday speech is uncanny, as in the poem "Ma Rainey":

I talked to a fellow, an' the fellow say
"She jes' catch hold of us, somekindaway.
She sang Backwater Blues one day:
An' den de folks, dey natchally bowed dey heads an' cried,
Bowed dey heavy heads, shet dey moufs up tight an' cried,
An Ma lef' de stage, an' followed some de folks outside."

Dere wasn't much more de fellow say.
She jes' gits hold of us dataway.[5]

Though he would publish no more volumes of poetry until *The Last Ride of Wild Bill and Eleven Narrative Poems* (1975), Brown published a number of pioneering works of literary criticism in the 1930s. These include *The Negro in American Fiction* (1937) and *Negro Poetry and Drama* (1937). Today, his literary reputation eclipses all the poets of the Harlem Renaissance except that of Hughes, even though

Arna Bontemps

his initial volume marked the end of the Harlem Renaissance era.

ARNA BONTEMPS

Like Claude McKay, James Weldon Johnson, and Langston Hughes, Arna Bontemps was a versatile writer of poetry and prose as well as an anthologist. His nonfiction works include many for young readers. He was born in Louisiana of a stonemason father and a schoolteacher mother, but moved to New York in 1923 and became a teacher. When the Renaissance was at its zenith, his poetry appeared in the magazines *Opportunity* and *Crisis*. However, his first novel, *God Sends Sunday* (1931), is considred the final novel of the Harlem Renaissance.

Black Sunday (1935) is a novel about a slave revolt in Virginia and *Drums at Dusk* (1939) is about a slave revolt in Haiti. Bontemps collaborated with Langston Hughes on *The Poetry of the Negro* (1949) and *The Book of Negro Folklore* (1958). For more than twenty years, Bontemps was the head librarian at Fisk University in Nashville, Tennessee.

FENTON JOHNSON

Only a very few black writers were published in the experimental modernist periodicals. Fenton Johnson (1888–1958) published in the avant-garde magazines *Poetry* and *Others*, in the early 1920s. Typical is a poem like "The Banjo Player":

There is music in me, the music of a peasant people.
I wander through the levee, picking my banjo and sing-
ing my songs of the cabin and the field. At the Last
Chance Saloon I am as welcome as the violets in
March; there is always food and drink for me there,
and the dimes of those who love honest music. Behind
the railroad tracks the little children clap their hands
and love me as they love Kris Kringle.
But I fear that I am a failure. Last night a woman called
me a troubadour. What is a troubadour?[6]

Though he compiled a book of poems in the 1930s, *The Daily Grind: 41 WPA Poems*, it sits to this day in a university library, unpublished. Johnson's reputation rests on some fifteen poems published in anthologies.

WOMEN POETS

Women poets of the Harlem Renaissance include Georgia Douglas Johnson, Anne Spenser, Jessie Fauset, Angelina Weld Grimke, Alice Dunbar-Nelson, Helene Johnson, Gwendolyn B. Bennett, Effie Lee Newsome, and Mae V. Cowdery. These poets and others are collected in the anthology edited by Maureen Honey, *Shadowed Dreams: Women's Poetry of the Harlem Renaissance*. Few of these poets published books. They are remembered today only through their appearance in the major anthologies of the period.

Georgia Douglas Johnson (1886–1966) published *The Heart of a Woman and Other Poems* (1918), with a foreword by William Stanley Braithwaite. That book was followed by *Bronze* (1922) and *An Autumn Love Cycle* (1928). She also published a one-act play, *Plumes* (1927). Her final collection is *Share My World: A Book of Poems* (1962), published when she was in her seventies.

Johnson was a distinguished civil servant as well as a poet, serving as commissioner of conciliation in the U.S. Department of Labor during the mid-1920s. Her Washington, D.C., home was a gathering place for poets, and most of the well-known writers of the Harlem Renaissance visited her while in the nation's capitol. Johnson published in the major Renaissance periodicals, *Crisis, Opportunity*, and elsewhere. She appears in the African-American poetry anthologies of the day.

The lesbian love poems of Mae V. Cowdery and Angelina Weld Grimke are pioneering efforts in American letters. Mae V. Cowdery (1909–53) came to the attention of the *Crisis* while in her early twenties. Though associated with the Harlem writers, she seems to have spent most of her life in Greenwich Village. She published one volume, *We Lift Our Voices and Other Poems* (1936), but otherwise remained obscure. She died a suicide.

Cowdery was one of the few Harlem poets who wrote consistently in a modernist, free verse style. Many of her best poems are full of lush imagery, or the frank sensuality of love poems like "Farewell":

No more
The feel of your hand
On my breast
Like the silver path
Of the moon
On dark heaving ocean.[7]

LITERARY GARVEYISM

Tony Martin's *Literary Garveyism* (1983) documents the extensive amount of literary publication in Garvey's *Negro World* newspaper, quoting from poems, book reviews, short fiction, and literary essays. Martin writes of poets Leonard I. Brathwaite, Ethel Trew Dunlap, Ernest E. Mair, J. R. Ralph Casimir, Lucian B. Watkins, and Augusta Savage, the well-known sculptor. The *Negro World* also published poems by the youthful Zora Neale Hurston, who was to make her reputation in the 1930s as a novelist.

Aside from Casimir, who is from Dominica and authored at least four books of verse, none of these poets published collections. Nonetheless, Martin shows that the literary world of Harlem extended far beyond the reach of the NAACP's *Crisis,* the Urban League's *Opportunity,* and A. Philip Randolph's *Messenger* magazines.

Of the major Harlem poets, both Langston Hughes and Countee Cullen remained without collected editions of their work for many decades. Finally, in the 1990s, two collections appeared: *My Soul's High Song: The Collected Writings of Countee Cullen* (1991), edited by Gerald Early, and *The Collected Poems of Langston Hughes* (1994), edited by Arnold Rampersad and David Roessel.

Claude McKay's posthumously published *Selected Poems* (1953) was supplemented by Wayne F. Cooper's *The Passion of Claude McKay: Selected Poetry and Prose, 1912–1948* (1973), but McKay's collected poems remain unpublished. "God's Trombones" remains in print, as does some of James Weldon Johnson's other poetry.

THREE

"Race" Music and American Music

The spring and summer of 1924 Langston Hughes worked in Paris as a waiter in several nightclubs, one of which, Le Grand Duc, featured a jazz band. Famous black musicians living in Paris would come into Le Grand Duc and play until the wee hours of the morning, among them pioneering jazz drummer Buddy Gilmore.

That autumn Hughes signed onto a merchant ship and, after a month-and-a-half-long voyage, docked in New Jersey on November 10. That same evening, Hughes went with his friend Countee Cullen to an NAACP benefit at Arthur "Happy" Rhone's nightclub in Harlem. The leaders of the NAACP were there: W. E. B. Du Bois, Walter White, Mary White Ovington, and James Weldon Johnson.

Both the old and new styles of African-American music were being performed that night. When Hughes walked in the door, Alberta Hunter was singing "Everybody Loves My Baby, But My Baby Don't Love Nobody But Me." Bill "Bojangles" Robinson,

Florence Mills

the greatest of tap dancers, was also on the bill. Noble Sissle (one of the writers of the big Broadway hit of 1921, *Shuffle Along*) and his orchestra, the Sizzling Syncopators, played the old style. The big star of the night was Florence Mills, a woman of extraordinary beauty and talent. A veteran of both the cabaret and theatrical stage, she had appeared in *Shuffle Along* and the *Plantation Review* and was on her way to further success in *Blackbirds of 1925* and *Blackbirds of 1926*. Though Mills left behind no recordings, she was the most loved entertainer in 1920s Harlem. When she died in 1927, some 150,000 people lined the streets for her funeral procession.

By combining the best aspects of the ragtime pianists, the syncopated orchestras, the classic blues singers, the New Orleans musicians, and the Tin Pan Alley music of Broadway, the African-American urban musicians had fashioned jazz. The Fletcher Henderson Orchestra, the first of the big bands, played the new style music, jazz. Among its members were saxophonists Don Redman, Buster Bailey, and Coleman Hawkins, and the great drummer Kaiser Marshall. Henderson, a pianist, was soon broadcasting nationwide on the new electronic medium, the radio. The band's latest addition to the trumpet section was a twenty-four-year-old trumpet player from New Orleans, Louis Armstrong.

After serving his apprenticeship in New Orleans, playing on Mississippi riverboats and at cabarets and social gatherings, Armstrong followed King Oliver's Creole Jazz Band to Chicago in 1922. By the time Armstrong linked up with Henderson in New York, he was already considered one of the greatest musicians in this fascinating music, jazz, that was to give its name to the 1920s.

King Oliver's Creole Jazz Band, Chicago, May 1923, Louis Armstong seated center.

Among the great practitioners of orchestral or "big band" jazz in Harlem were Cabell "Cab" Calloway, James Melvin "Jimmy" Lunceford, William "Chick" Webb, Earl Hines (based mainly in Chicago), and Fletcher Henderson. But the greatest of them all was Edward Kennedy "Duke" Ellington, a pianist from Washington, D.C., whose father had worked as a butler in the White House.

Duke Ellington got his start playing in a basement club in Manhattan's Times Square, The Hollywood, later known as The Kentucky Club. The band, then called the Washingtonians, was working to develop its own unique style. Ellington did so by taking a

47

Louis Armstrong

page out of Fletcher Henderson's book. To get the "hot" sound that dancers were looking for, Henderson had found Louis Armstrong. Ellington found Bubber Miley. James Wesley Miley (1903–32), a trumpeter, "was raised on soul and saturated and marinated in soul," wrote Ellington many years later in his autobiography, *Music Is My Mistress.* "Every note he played was filled with the pulse of compulsion."[1] Miley was the stellar example of the hot jazz trumpeter. His ability to conjure up the strangest sounds made the Ellington band unique. Other musicians in the band included Johnny Hodges on alto saxophone, trombonist Joe "Tricky Sam" Nanton, and drummer Sonny Greer.

By the late 1920s, Harlem had become a haven for prohibition-era (white) gangsters, who opened uptown clubs for the downtown tourist trade. The Cotton Club was the most famous of these clubs. Next was Barron Wilkins' Exclusive Club which was a black-owned club. Almost every important black pianist in New York had been hired by Wilkins at one time or another. Duke Ellington's first big Harlem engagement was at Wilkins'.

The place was frequented by "big spenders, gamblers, sportsmen, and women, all at the peak of their professions. People would come in who would ask for change for a C-note in half-dollar pieces," Ellington wrote in *Music Is My Mistress.*[2] (A "C-note" is a $100 bill.) At the end of a song, the patrons would throw the coins up in the air. They would land on the dance floor, Ellington recalled, "and make a jingling fanfare for the prosperity of our tomorrow."

At Smalls, waiters danced the Charleston while balancing packed trays on their fingertips. At Connie's Inn, the big cabaret revues could be seen, like Fats Waller and Andy Razaf's *Keep Shufflin'* and *Hot Chocolates.* These revues also ran as theater productions on Broadway. They introduced such popular songs as "Ain't Misbehavin" and "What Did I Do to

Duke Ellington Orchestra

Be So Black and Blue," both among Razaf and
Waller's most famous songs.

Most nights at Connie's, the musicians and waiters
were the only blacks in the place. The club's policy
was "white" customers only. In the middle of Harlem.
And it wasn't the only club with that policy, either.
The Cotton Club also didn't allow black patrons. It
didn't matter that Jack Johnson, the black boxing
champ, was a partner in the club. Its main owner was
a bootlegger, murderer, and gangster named Owney
Madden. For the upper-class whites and show business people who patronized the club, this was part of
its charm. According to Langston Hughes, the Cotton

Club was a Jim Crow club for gangsters and monied whites. They were not cordial to Negro patronage, unless you were a celebrity.

Duke Ellington in late 1927 began his four-year residence at the Cotton Club. There he developed the repertoire for which he became world famous: "Black and Tan Fantasy," "Mood Indigo," "East St. Louis Toodle-oo," and his homage to Florence Mills, "Black Beauty."

The "jungle music" played by Ellington's Jungle Band was about the wildest played in the 1920s. Trumpeter Bubber Miley was a "growl specialist" because of his mastery in playing the muted trumpet. Joe "Tricky Sam" Nanton was another whose style came close to sounding like an hysterical voice. Even today a song like "East St. Louis Toodle-oo" or "Black and Tan Fantasy" can stun the uninitiated.

Ellington rode to great fame as a result of this engagement. By 1930, he was considered important enough to accompany a group of distinguished blacks on an official visit to President Herbert Hoover's White House. He broadcast nationally on radio every day. By the time he gave up his Cotton Club residency in February 1931, he was a famous man and the Cotton Club was the most famous nightclub in the world.

THE BLUES

Cincinnati-born Mamie Smith was a cabaret singer who had traveled around the country with various vaudeville-type revues when she met pianist Perry Bradford sometime in 1920. By then she'd made a name for herself, singing in cabarets that catered to black people. In late 1920, she was in a show at the Lincoln Theater, *Maid of Harlem,* and one of the

Duke Ellington

songs she sang there, written by Mississippi-born Bradford, was "Harlem Blues."

The blues music of the black rural south wasn't too well known then, outside its native territory. Early versions of the blues, especially those associated with composer W. C. Handy, had caught on with the public. Handy's best known compositions were "St. Louis Blues," "Beale Street Blues," and "Memphis Blues." Though they showed the definite influence of the rural music, Handy often composed "blues" that were little more than southern versions of the syncopated, ragtime-influenced music already popular with dance and concert orchestras in New York. Though itinerant singers had performed the country music for years in traveling shows, musicians who played at dances and concerts in New York—many of whom were born and grew up in northern cities—were ignorant of the blues.

The mass migration of black people from the South brought with it singers and musicians too. It was just a matter of time, in those months after the end of World War I, before one of them would be the catalyst through which this new music would catch on. Mamie Smith was that catalyst.

In August 1920, with a band led by pianist Willie "The Lion" Smith in OK recording studio in New York, Mamie Smith recorded "Crazy Blues," a Perry Bradford composition, and "It's Right Here For You (If You Don't Come Get It—'T'aint No Fault of Mine)," two 78-rpm, three-minute disks. "We got twenty-five dollars apiece for the two sides," recalled pianist Smith. "And no royalty." The records were released in November 1920. "In no time at all it was selling like hot cakes in Harlem," writes Willie "The Lion" Smith in *Music On My Mind*.[3] The tune, he added, was "just an ordinary blues strain" that several Harlem composers and pianists claimed as their own. Nevertheless, within weeks, seventy-five thousand disks sold on the streets of Harlem. The record company executives couldn't believe it. The blues had finally arrived, and made Mamie Smith a star.

Bessie Smith, a great and popular blues artist, especially with black people, also had a profound influence on African-American literary artists. Black writers have used Smith's music as both inspiration and as a tool for creating art. Langston Hughes' first book, *The Weary Blues*, contains the poet's early attempts at putting the blues down on paper. James Baldwin, retreating to an isolated village in Switzerland to finish his first novel in the mid-1950s, took a stack of Bessie Smith records with him for company. One of the most moving tributes in African-American literature to any musician is poet Robert Hayden's *Homage to the Empress of the Blues.*

Her first record, "Down Hearted Blues," for Columbia records, was released in June 1923. By then, American record companies had discovered the African-American market and were fast developing whole divisions to market to them. New Orleans pianist and composer ("Baby Won't You Please Come Home") Clarence Williams (1898–1965), who served as talent scout, brought her to Columbia.

RACE RECORDS

Record companies were marketing artists like Smith as "race" singers, and developing whole "race record" catalogs. "Race" music was big business and the designation, "race," was not necessarily seen as negative by African-American consumers. The same race consciousness that produced the Harlem Renaissance also allowed black consumers to see products like phonograph records, that were especially designated for them, in a positive light.

In 1922, William Christopher Handy (1873–1958), composer of "St. Louis Blues," one of the most-recorded blues songs of all time, and partner Harry Pace started the Black Swan record company, the first African-American-owned record company. The company advertised: "The Only Genuine Colored Record. The Others Are Only Passing For Colored."

54

Bessie Smith

Ethel Waters and Trixie Smith recorded for Black Swan. Fletcher Henderson, who later accompanied Smith on several of her more famous records, was Black Swan's recording manager. W. E. B. Du Bois was on the company's board of directors, and its music director was the famous African-American classical music composer and arranger William Grant Still.

The Black Swan record company reflected the conflicting cultural sentiments of the black leadership at that time. While recording Ethel Waters' version of "Down Home Blues," the company also recorded operatic arias. Among it's notable actions was rejecting Bessie Smith, who auditioned for the label before she signed with Columbia. The label's sales were dismal, and Pace sold the catalog to Paramount in 1923.

BROADWAY MUSICAL THEATER

The collaboration between composers Noble Sissle and Eubie Blake brought modern black music to Broadway. *Shuffle Along* was praised by a New York critic as a breeze of super-jazz blown up from Dixie soon after it opened on Broadway in May 1921. Many of its songs became classics; its most famous, "I'm Just Wild About Harry," became President Harry Truman's 1948 campaign song. *Shuffle Along* produced beautiful songs such as "Love Will Find a Way," recorded by Sissle and Blake for the Emerson label the month following its opening, and "Gypsy Blues," recorded by the Paul Whiteman orchestra five months after the show opened.

Sissle and Blake wrote the show with the comedy-writing team of Flournoy Miller and Aubrey Lyles, a pair of former Fisk University students whom the songwriting team met in 1920 at an NAACP fund-raiser. The show had a number of great African-American musical and theatrical people in it. Its leading lady was Lottie Gee, a veteran of several Cole and Johnson productions; Paul Robeson, Josephine Baker, Fredi Washington, and Florence Mills were in the chorus; and Hall Johnson and William Grant Still were in the orchestra. All these people became famous African-American artists, and Robeson, Baker, and Mills were each figures in the Harlem Renaissance.

JAZZ IDIOM IN LITERATURE

"Let us invent an idiom for the proper transposition of jazz into words!" wrote poet Hart Crane in 1922.[4] Crane was part of a circle of writers associated with magazines such as *Broom, Succession, Double Dealer, S 4 N*, and *The Little Review*. Both Jean Toomer and Crane found in jazz a great source of inspiration. As Crane himself exclaimed, the aim of many modern literary artists of the 1920s was to emulate jazz. When he finished "The Marriage of Faustus and Helen," one of his major poems, he wrote a friend that the jazz rhythms in that first verse were something he had been wishing to do for many a day.

Everything avant-garde in that decade was associated with jazz. Poets like T. S. Eliot, William Carlos Williams, Wallace Stevens, and e. e. cummings were considered by critics to be jazz disciples. The "free verse" movement in early twentieth century English language poetry can be traced partially to the freer rhythms heard first in ragtime, and then in jazz. The Dada and Surrealist poets, painters, and sculptors in France cited jazz as an example of the sort of art they were aiming to achieve.

Nonsense, noise, and other elements in African-American music were seized upon by modernist artists in Europe and America. European composers including Igor Stravinsky, Darius Milhaud, Anton Dvorak, Eric Satie, and the American George Antheil, whose *Ballet Mecanique* (1925) caused a mini-riot in Paris, were all influenced by the rhythmical and noise elements in jazz. They in turn influenced the post-1960 avant-garde jazz styles of musicians like Albert Ayler, John Coltrane, Anthony Braxton, the Art Ensemble of Chicago, David Murray, and others.

A song Armstrong recorded in the winter of 1926, "Heebie Jeebies," is the first example of what would later be called "scat" singing, wordless nonsense vocals. In a sense, Armstrong would reverse Hart Crane's desire to transpose jazz into words by creating a wordless nonsense art. Innovations like Armstrong's on "Heebie Jeebies" made many of the avant-garde claim jazz as a kindred spirit.

French composer Darius Milhaud's most famous composition, *La Creation Du Monde* (1923), is deeply influenced by jazz, and some of the melodies sound very familiar to anyone who has heard Joe Oliver's Creole Jazz Band's recording of "Southern Stomp." Oliver's recording was made in Chicago in September 1923. Milhaud's composition had it's premier in Paris the next month. These two musical first cousins show just how far the influence of jazz had penetrated into world culture.

FOUR

The Novels of the Harlem Renaissance

Although there were few novels in print by black authors when the Harlem Renaissance began, a rich heritage of African-American prose existed. The works of Paul Dunbar, Charles Chestnutt, and Frances E. W. Harper were pioneering works that reached an appreciative audience. Ironically, some of the richest African-American literature, the slave narratives, were not recognized as literature at all. In his survey of literature in the Harlem Renaissance anthology, *The New Negro*, William Stanley Braithwaite, the black critic, dismissed the slave narrative of the nineteenth century as a negligible contribution. Yet these autobiographies of escaped slaves were forerunners of the first person narrative of the twentieth century. With their searing "I was there" quality, they have influenced African-American writers from Booker T. Washington to Ralph Ellison, Malcolm X, Toni Morrison, and more.

Charles W. Chestnutt (1858–1932) was the first African-American novelist to reach a large, white audience. The dilemmas related to "passing" for white and other problems of racial identity are among his themes. With remarkable sympathy he explored the social and emotional problems of that group which is descended from both slaves and masters. At the same time, he was critical of the assimilationist tendencies common among lighter-skinned African-Americans.

In one of his most famous stories, "The Wife of His Youth," Chestnutt depicts a man who, after entering exclusive mulatto society, is found by the dark-skinned wife he married during slavery. The hero's decision to reunite with his long-lost wife illustrates what Chestnutt saw as African-Americans' unity across the color spectrum. Chestnutt's novel, *The House Behind the Cedars* (1900) is his most famous book. Chestnutt received the NAACP's Spingarn Medal in 1928.

Between 1905, the date of Chestnutt's last novel, *The Colonel's Dream*, and 1920, only a few novels by African-Americans were published, including: W. E. B. Du Bois' *The Quest of the Silver Fleece* (1911), Sutton E. Griggs' *Pointing the Way*, and James Weldon Johnson's *The Autobiography of an Ex-Coloured Man*. Johnson's novel was published anonymously in 1912 and not issued under the author's name until 1927.

THE MIDDLE-CLASS MULATTO NOVEL

The most acclaimed creative prose work of the Harlem Renaissance is *Cane* (1923) by Jean Toomer. *Cane*, a semi-autobiographical collage of stories, sketches, and poems, is regarded as one of the most unique American novels of the 1920s.

JEAN TOOMER

Jean Toomer (1894–1967) was a part of the "revolution of the word," the literary experimentation of

60

Jean Toomer

artists and writers who sought to use hallucination, dreams, spontaneity, and the unconscious as artistic sources. He was close friends with poets Hart Crane and Edna St. Vincent Millay and the writer Waldo Frank, and he published in the same magazines as Ezra Pound and T. S. Eliot. Parts of *Cane* were published in *The Little Review*, which just a few years earlier had serialized James Joyce's *Ulysses*.

Toomer was also deeply rooted in African-American history. His grandfather, P. B. S. Pinchback, had been governor of Louisiana briefly during Reconstruction (making him, along with Virginia governor L. Douglas Wilder, who served from 1989 to 1993, one of two African-American state governors in United States history). Toomer grew up in his grandfather's home, part of the mulatto elite of Washington, D.C., at the turn of the century. Although his relatives identified themselves as Negroes, Toomer's mixed-race heritage seems to have caused him lifelong anxiety, a tension that animates *Cane*.

CANE

Unlike a conventional novel, *Cane* has no plot. It is a record of events in the growth of a consciousness. Each sketch, poem, or story is a variation on a common theme—the race consciousness of urban and rural African-Americans just before the massive migration to the cities changed black American life forever. The settings of the prose pieces in *Cane* shift from rural Georgia to Washington, D.C., and Chicago.

From the opening story—a scene, really,—describing a young girl, Karintha, the whole first section is a love song to black women. Even the section's concluding tale, "Blood-Burning Moon," with its horrifyingly detailed description of a lynching, is a story of a love triangle involving a black woman.

The stories in the second section, which take place in Washington and Chicago, focus on middle-class mulattos. These stories and sketches of unrequited love raise enduring questions—What is "race"? What does it mean to be "black" or "white"?

The story, "Kabnis," the third and final section, chronicles a northern-born and bred African-American schoolteacher's experiences in a rural southern com-

Jean Toomer and his bride, Marjory Latimer

munity. It is based on Toomer's own experiences as a teacher in Georgia.

The structure of *Cane* is remarkable in the way it mixes genres of prose and poetry and effortlessly shifts narrative point of view. *Cane* has much in common with other mixed-genre texts of the time like poet William Carlos Williams' *Spring and All* (1923). The theme, the problem of racial identity for mixed-race people in a racist society, has long been popular with African-American writers. It would eventually drive Toomer out of literature and out of African-American life. The pressure of the conflicts raised by this question proved too much for Toomer, and he eventually "passed," living as a white man, claiming an identity as a nonracialized American.

NELLA LARSEN

The same theme is also found in the work of Nella Larsen (1891–1964), the daughter of a Danish mother and a black West Indian father. Larsen's two novels, *Quicksand* (1928) and *Passing* (1929), received much praise when they were published. In 1930 Larsen became the first African-American woman to receive a Guggenheim Fellowship in creative writing, to research a third novel in France and Spain. After 1930 Larsen disappeared from the literary scene. She spent most of the last thirty-five years of her life working as a nurse in several New York hospitals.

Both novels are studies of African-American middle-class life in the years following World War I. Larsen's characters are, like Toomer's, from the small black elite. It's a modest elite. The most exalted person in any of the books by these black writers is a doctor or a descendent of a Reconstruction politician whose family might still, in the early 1920s, receive Republican patronage favors.

The heroine of *Quicksand*, Helga Crane, has a Danish mother and a black father. Crane's adventures in Chicago, Denmark, Harlem, and the Deep South do not lead to happiness.

In *Passing*, the choice many light-skinned African-Americans faced is explored through the lives of two women: one, Irene Redfield, marries a dark-skinned African-American doctor; the other, Claire Kendry, passes for white and marries a white man who is a vicious racist. In all such books, the mulatto finds no solace in becoming a fraud by crossing the color line into the "white" world. Larsen's books are remark-

Nella Larsen (second from left) receives Harmon Award from Miss Harmon (left). Also present are (left to right) Channing Tobins, James Weldon Johnson, and Dr. George Haynes. (Last person not identified)

able for their consideration of the meaning of race and identity in a racist society.

BLACK WORKING-CLASS NOVELS

At the other end of the spectrum are the more notorious Harlem novels. Two, *The Blacker the Berry* by Wallace Thurman (1929) and *Home to Harlem* by Claude McKay (1928), are polar opposites of the middle-class mulatto novels. Thurman, who had been associated with the Garvey movement, had a sharp wit, a keen sense of detail, and a clean, spare prose style. In *The Blacker the Berry*, Emma Lou Morgan, a black-hued African-American woman, is ashamed of her blackness. Thurman describes in detail the shame his heroine carries with her everywhere. In Harlem, she works as a maid to a white actress who plays a mulatto on stage, and has a series of unsatisfactory romances.

Aside from some picturesque scenes of Harlem life, most of the action in *The Blacker the Berry* is of less consequence than the turbulent emotions going on inside Emma Lou. By the end, she realizes that her feelings about her self-image have helped lead to unhappiness. The author's race pride—signified by the book's title—is clear. The book explores the psychology of self respect and dignity as well as pride in one's own blackness.

CLAUDE MCKAY

Claude McKay was a leading poet of the Harlem Renaissance and his novels *Home to Harlem* (1928) and *Banjo* (1929) remain classics about the working class. *Home to Harlem* sees life from the point of view of its lead character Jake Brown, who works in the kitchen of a passenger railroad car (as did the author). The book is full of parties and music. The approximations of blues lyrics set the tone, propelling a tale of the hero's adventures in life and love, while touching on issues like trade unionism, world literature, the comparative merits of life for black people in America and Europe, and the common everyday problems of working on the job.

Claude McKay spent the fall and winter of 1922 to 1923 in Russia. The Russian Revolution had taken place in 1917, and the original leaders of that earth-shattering event, Lenin and Trotsky, were still heading the revolutionary government. McKay had become one of the first post-World War I black socialist intellectuals, due in large part to his stint as associate editor of *The Liberator* in New York.

He went to revolutionary Russia to attend the congress of the Communist International in Moscow, where he was lionized by communist leaders. He helped shape the communist movement's policy against racism and colonialism—a policy that would remain unchanged for decades.

Despite his full participation in these early communist policy debates, McKay never became a disciplined party member. He early rejected the authoritarian aspects of the Bolshevik regime, even while agreeing with many of its policies. Besides, McKay was a creative writer and rejected any authority that would presume to tamper with the artist's freedom. After he left Russia in the spring of 1923 (and having authored one of the first books on African-Americans published in the Soviet Union), he went to Germany and then to France.

He arrived in Paris in August 1923. His arrival, McKay's biographer writes, had been noted in the Paris edition of the *New York Herald Tribune* by Eugene Jolas. Jolas was a poet and an editor of the magazine *Transition*, which published in serial form James Joyce's last and most obscure novel, *Finnegans Wake.* Jolas wrote that McKay was writing a novel about his American and Jamaican experiences.

McKay stayed in Paris until January of the following year, when he went to Marseilles, France's oldest seaport, the setting for his second novel, *Banjo,* which solidified his international literary reputation. McKay's novels would become much more influential in world literature than his poetry. He spent a decade in Europe and North Africa, writing *Home to Harlem* (1928); *Banjo* (1929); his volume of short stories, *Gingertown* (1932); and his last novel, *Banana Bottom* (1933).

McKay's influence would be strongest on the international African literary scene, especially among French-speaking African and Caribbean writers like poet Leon Damas, poet and longtime president of Senegal Leopold Senghor, and Martiniquean poet and politician Aime Cesaire. Senghor considered Claude McKay the veritable inventor of *Negritude*...not of the word...but of the values of *Negritude*. McKay wrote about the international black world, the 1920s and 1930s dockworkers and sailors in cities like Marseilles, who traveled from Harlem to Paris to Hamburg carrying the international cargo of the developed world. In this, he was the first to create in literature a genuine "Pan-African" sensibility. This sensibility is alive today in New York and in most European cities, as immigrants from Africa transform the old colonial civilizations.

McKay lived most of his life abroad in poverty, struggling to create his novels. He returned to the United States in 1933, in the middle of the Great Depression. By then, the market for his fiction, and for most writing by the black authors of the Harlem Renaissance, had dried up. McKay spent his remaining years in New York in relative obscurity.

McKay's characters were quite realistic, with all of humanity's flaws. That didn't go down too well with middle-class blacks like Du Bois, who distinctly disliked *Home to Harlem*. He reviewed both *Quicksand* and *Home to Harlem* together in the June 1928 issue of the *Crisis*. He liked Larsen's novel, though. Larsen, he wrote "has seized an interesting character and fitted her into a close yet delicately woven plot." He added: "White folk will not like this book. It is not near nasty enough for New York columnists."[1]

Of McKay's tale of partying, working-class Harlemites with their coarse language and (presumably) coarser ways, Du Bois wrote, "it nauseates me, and after the dirtier parts of its filth I feel distinctly like taking a bath."[2]

What made these books different was a focus on the black working-class, and on the emergent Harlem nightlife with its cabarets and jazz bands. These books were sharply criticized in their time and suffer from critical neglect to this day. They reflect the conflicts that have plagued the African-American community about "proper" versus "lowlife" culture from the days of Bessie Smith to the hip-hop era.

Some leaders of Harlem's intelligentsia didn't like the "lowlife" theme. They were embarrassed by the frank treatment of intragroup color consciousness in *The Blacker the Berry*, and the realistic portrayal of cabarets, rent parties, gambling, and sex in both Thurman's novel and in *Home to Harlem*. It didn't help, either, that one of the first of these— and one of the most popular—"Harlem" novels was written by a white man.

CARL VAN VECHTEN

Carl Van Vechten was a journalist—chief music critic for one of the big New York daily newspapers. He brought Langston Hughes and Knopf, the New York publishing firm, together. In 1926 Van Vechten published a novel, *Nigger Heaven*, that went through nine printings in four months (in contrast to *Cane*, its first printing selling only 500 copies).

The book's title refers to the racially segregated balcony in a theater. It was offensive to many, including Countee Cullen, who refused to speak to Van Vechten for years. W. E. B. Du Bois hated the book as well.

But Langston Hughes loved it. He "had found the novel, if anything, too pro-Negro," writes the poet's biographer Arnold Rampersad in *The Life of Langston Hughes*. Nella Larsen and James Weldon Johnson thought highly of the book because, they said, it truthfully portrayed African-American and Harlem life.

Later critics and historians cite *Nigger Heaven* as an inspiration for the Harlem novels written by blacks.

RUDOLPH FISHER

Another Harlem novel of the period that uses working-class characters is the humorous *The Walls of Jericho* by Harlem hospital doctor Rudolph Fisher. Fisher's characters, like McKay's, also like to party. And the humor in *The Walls of Jericho* shouldn't blind the reader to its intent as a serious literary work. Unlike *Home to Harlem*, however, Fisher's book doesn't try to tell its story from the point of view of its working-class heroes. As sympathetic as he is to his characters, the moving men Jinx Jenkins and Bubber Brown, Fisher is also very busy laughing at them in a way that McKay is not. For that reason, *The Walls of Jericho* sometimes veers very close to caricature. Ultimately, it is saved by the author's keen sense of humor.

ZORA NEALE HURSTON

Novelist and folklorist Zora Neale Hurston was a student of Georgia Douglas Johnson and Alain Locke at Howard University. She moved to New York City and from 1925 to 1927, while studying at Barnard College she became acquainted with all the leading artists of the Harlem Renaissance. She published

Zora Neale Hurston

stories in *Negro World, The Messenger, Opportunity,* and *World Tomorrow* magazines, and was an editorial member of the single issue magazine *Fire!!,* published by several of the younger literary personalities of the Renaissance.

During the late 1920s and early 1930s she worked as an anthropologist, having studied under the great anthropologist Franz Boas at Barnard. She traveled throughout the South collecting folktales, rituals, and other oral traditions of the black South. Her first book, *Mules and Men*, an anthropological study of African-American spiritualist ritual, was written in 1930 and published in 1935. One of the first books of its kind written by an African-American, it tells of her adventures on her southern field trips. *Tell My Horse* documents her travels to Jamaica and Haiti.

Hurston wrote her first novel, *Jonah's Gourd Vine*, in 1934, in just two months. Her most famous work is the novel *Their Eyes Were Watching God* (1937) set in the all-black community of Eatonville, Florida (where Hurston grew up). Hurston's tale of Janie Crawford's search for true love with a man who respects her humanity explores the meaning of social equality between the sexes. Hurston published a total of seven books, including an autobiography, becoming the most prolific African-American woman writer of the mid-century.

Though she died in obscurity, Hurston's work was rediscovered in the 1970s, and has enjoyed a tremendous reputation since. She is an inspiration to a wide range of African-American writers, most prominently the 1985 Pulitzer Prize-winning novelist Alice Walker.

In all, twenty-six novels were published by Harlem Renaissance writers. They include *Crisis* literary editor Jessie Fauset's *There Is Confusion, Plum Bun* (1929), and *The Chinaberry Tree* (1931); NAACP official Walter White's two novels, *Fire in the Flint* (1924) and *Flight* (1926); W. E. B. Du Bois' *Dark Princess* (1928); Wallace Thurman's *Infants of the Spring* (1932);

Countee Cullen's *One Way to Heaven* (1932); Langston Hughes' *Not Without Laughter* (1930); Rudolph Fisher's second novel, *The Conjure-Man Dies* (1932), which is considered the first detective novel written by an African-American; and George Schuyler's *Black No More* (1931). No comprehensive study of American literature in the 1920s is possible without taking the fiction of the black writers into account.

FIVE

Theater

For most of the nineteenth century, serious theater performed by African-Americans in New York was done by small companies. Not until the final years of the century did black stage performers begin to reach large audiences with nonminstrel musical comedy shows. *Oriental America* (1896) was the first black show to play Broadway proper; *A Trip to Coontown* (1889–98) was the first musical to be entirely produced by African-Americans.

In the summer of 1898, composer Will Marion Cook and poet Paul Lawrence Dunbar collaborated on *Clorindy—The Origin of the Cakewalk.* Cook called it an operetta. On opening night, at the Casino Roof Garden, when he entered the orchestra pit there were only about fifty people on the Roof. When they finished the opening chorus, the house was packed to suffocation. What had happened, Cook remembered many years later, was that the show downstairs was letting out. The audience heard those heavenly Negro voices and took to the elevators.

The opening chorus was an orchestral and choral arrangement of Cook's "Darktown Is Out Tonight." The song consisted of complicated rhythm and bold harmonies, and was very taxing on the voice, Cook remembered. The show, according to James Weldon Johnson, was the talk of New York. It was the first demonstration of the possibilities of syncopated Negro music. Cook was the first competent composer to take what was then known as ragtime and work it out in a musicianly way. He was also, no doubt, the first to use syncopated music in a musical stage show. Along with J. Rosamond Johnson, Bob Cole, and others, Cook, and his troupe were pioneers in American musical theater.

The greatest of all black pioneers was the comedy team of Bert Williams and George Walker. For eleven years beginning in 1896, they thrilled theatrical audiences in New York and elsewhere. Among their biggest hits was *In Dahomey* (1903), which opened in the heart of New York's theater district in Times Square and then traveled to London where it gave a royal command performance at Buckingham Palace that summer. *In Abyssinia* (1906) and *Bandanna Land* (1907) were both hits also. The last show was the end of the Williams and Walker team, as Walker retired from the stage for health reasons.

Both *In Dahomey* and *In Abyssinia* were comedies set in Africa, in which Williams and Walker play characters who get themselves in and out of trouble. In *Bandanna Land* the pair of comics set their antics in the southern United States. All three shows were tremendous commercial and critical successes. After *Bandanna Land*, Williams performed as a single for several years. In 1910, he joined Florenz Ziegfeld's *Follies*, one of the most popular vaudeville companies.

*The comedy team of Bert Williams (left) and
George Walker*

He rose to even higher fame, remaining there until
his death at forty-six in 1922.

Bert Williams was an important transitional figure
in African-American theater. Considered one of the

funniest comedians who ever lived, his humor remains fresh on records he made over seventy years ago. But there remains the self-denigrating minstrel tradition from which Williams emerged and which can dull contemporary ears to the artistry in his work. To contemporary African-American sensibilities, Williams' act may produce feelings ranging from annoyance to chagrin in the way it uses racist stereotypes as sources for its humor. Yet ultimately a dignity comes through. Like other performers, Williams often performed in blackface. For many performers in vaudeville, black and white, it was virtually a requirement, yet it was terribly demeaning. Blackface comedy played on the most vicious racist stereotypes that portrayed African-Americans as stupid and lazy. But it was so ingrained in American theater that no one, it seemed, could escape it. Eubie Blake's biographer cites Blake as asserting that there was a time when even big stars like Al Jolson and Eddie Cantor had to use blackface or vanish into show business obscurity.

The African Theater, a permanent black theater company in New York in the early 1820s, produced serious drama, notably Shakespeare's *Othello*. A century later a troupe called the Colored Players performed three plays by white poet Ridgely Torrence at a small theater in Madison Square Garden. *The Rider of Dreams, Granny Maumee,* and *Simon the Cyrenian* were the first original plays to break decisively with the pattern of stereotypes and dehumanization that had plagued blacks in the theater for so long. The plays opened April 5, 1917, just one day before the United States entered World War I. War fever killed the plays, but not their historic importance.

In 1919 at the Cort Theater, Charles Gilpin appeared in John Drinkwater's *Abraham Lincoln*. Gilpin went on to originate the title role in Eugene O'Neill's *The Emperor Jones* at the Provincetown Playhouse in 1920. O'Neill would later say that of all the actors he had worked with (and O'Neill worked with some of the greatest), only three managed to realize the characters as he originally saw them, and Gilpin was one of them.

Gilpin and several other African-American actors of the early 1920s came out of African-American theater companies, notably the Lafayette Players and the Lincoln Theater group. These companies thrived in the nineteen-teens, presenting standard melodramas and serious plays, including Shakespearian drama like *Othello*. The Krigwa Players, a short-lived troupe, had the backing of, among others, W. E. B. Du Bois. The companies produced a large number of African-American artists who went on to careers on stage and screen. Performers like Inez Clough, Opal Cooper, Frank Wilson, Rose McClendon, Jules Bledsoe, Clarence Muse, and Leigh Whipper all started out in these Harlem stock theater companies, and would become relatively well-known actors.

SHUFFLE ALONG

Eubie Blake (1883–1983) and his partner, Noble Sissle (1889–1975), who created *Shuffle Along*, were the first big-time black performers to achieve stage success without using blackface. Their partners in *Shuffle Along*, Flournoy Miller and Aubrey Lyles, used blackface in their routines and in *Shuffle Along*. But by the early 1920s, Sissle and Blake were an established singer-songwriter team in their own right, and they had succeeded without the demeaning black cork makeup. The rejection of blackface by Sissle and Blake reflected the new militancy among black people. Until then, theatrical producers, who were white,

Charles Gilpin received an acting award for his role as the Emperor Jones, but at the close of the successful show he had to return to running an elevator.

believed that white audiences couldn't accept black performers in any role other than that of an absurd self-loathing clown, and black performers had to play to white stereotypes in order to work.

Sissle and Blake also changed things by broadening the subject matter of their songs, including love songs (which had been forbidden to black performers up until then). This new face of black performance made *Shuffle Along* quite a big deal when it opened in the summer of 1921. Coupled with the fact that no black production had appeared on Broadway in several years, *Shuffle Along* signaled a new era of black theater, another facet of the Harlem Renaissance.

The most popular African-American theatrical shows of the 1920s were the musical reviews that grew out of the success of *Shuffle Along*. There was *Strut Miss Lizzie* and *Seven-Eleven* (1922); *Liza* (1923); *Dixie to Broadway* (1924) starring Florence Mills; *Runnin Wild* (1924), a show by Miller and Lyles that helped introduce the Charleston, the dance with which the "jazz age" became most widely identified; *Chocolate Dandies* (1925), another show starring Florence Mills and written by Sissle and Blake; *Blackbirds* of 1926, arguably Mills' biggest hit show (it would be her last—she died the next year); *Africana* (1927) starring Ethel Waters, and *Keep Shuffling* (1928), a Miller and Lyles follow-up to their big hit.

In 1929 Thomas "Fats" Waller, one of the few Harlemites of that time who actually was born there, had his first big hit with *Hot Chocolates*. With his partner, Andy Razaf, he produced a number of fine songs including one that's sung to this day: "Ain't Misbehavin'."

PAUL ROBESON

Paul Robeson was the embodiment of the New Negro that emerged in the 1920s. In the spring of 1924 New Yorkers were getting their first glimpse of the twenty-six-year-old Paul Robeson starring in *All God's Chillen Got Wings* and *The Emperor Jones* at the

The Lafayette theater in Harlem. The marquee reads "Colored Musical Revues."

Provincetown Playhouse in Greenwich Village. Both plays written by Eugene O'Neill would help make Robeson's reputation.

His first film, *Body and Soul,* was directed by the African-American filmmaker Oscar Micheaux in 1924. Robeson, who starred in several motion pictures, including the film version of O'Neill's *The Emperor Jones* (1933), struggled for many years to find dignified parts to play in a film industry pervaded by extreme racist stereotyping.

Paul Robeson as the Emperor Jones

Robeson sang in a male quartet, The Four Harmony Kings, in *Shuffle Along*, the breakthrough show that revived African-American theater on Broadway. Besides doing pioneering work on stage

82

and screen, Robeson was also a singer and influential political leader. Although he wasn't the first to bring African-American spirituals to the concert stage, he sang them with an authority and power unmatched by any other singer of his generation.

Paul Robeson's appropriation of the old spirituals and songs from slavery days for the modern concert stage appealed to the avant-garde. (Langston Hughes was doing the same with the blues and aphorisms of rural and urban working-class African-Americans.) Robeson turned these "folk" artifacts into "high" art, forcing them to carry modern messages despite the intentions of those who originated these songs. He made this "folk" music a purely twentieth century creation.

Robeson opened the London production of O'Neill's *The Emperor Jones* in September 1925. In New York the next year he was in Jim Tully and Frank Dazey's *Black Boy* (based loosely on the life of Jack Johnson). In March 1928 he replaced the famous black tenor Jules Bledsoe in the DuBoise and Dorothy Heywood musical *Porgy*. He then performed a spectacular ten-month run in London in *Show Boat*. Robeson only had to sing one song, but it would be one forever identified with him: "Old Man River." In later years, Robeson changed the song's original words from those of a slave resigned to work to a worker protesting harsh conditions.

Robeson concluded the decade with two more successes. First, he starred in an experimental film made by the American imagist poet H. D. (Hilda Doolittle) and a group of her friends in Switzerland. *Borderline* (1930) is considered a classic among experimental films. Following that film, he returned to London to star in his most famous role, *Othello*.

Paul Robeson as Shakespeare's Othello. The production played 296 performances on Broadway.

After World War II Paul Robeson was forbidden by the U.S. government to go abroad because of his political views. He had to wage a nearly decade-long struggle to have his passport returned to him. When he succeeded, the triumphant five-year tour of Europe he embarked upon was his last. He retired to near seclusion after returning to the United States in 1963, his health broken. He died in 1976.

THE DRAMATIST LANGSTON HUGHES

Although his first plays weren't performed until the 1930s, Hughes' involvement in both dramatic and musical theater was extensive. His first professionally produced play was *Mulatto*, which opened on Broadway in 1935 with Rose McClendon. Hughes founded the Harlem Suitcase Theater in 1937. It produced his one-act play, *Don't You Want to Be Free*, which ran on weekends for 135 performances, for many years the longest-running play in Harlem history. He wrote many more plays that were performed by the Gilpin Players at the Karamu House in Cleveland. He collaborated with Zora Neale Hurston on *Mule Bone*.

Surprisingly few of Hughes' plays have been published. There exists one volume, *Five Plays by Langston Hughes*, which includes *Mulatto* as originally written (the Broadway version was rewritten and overly sensationalized by its producer), plus *Tambourines to Glory, Soul Gone Home, Little Ham*, and *Simply Heavenly*. This volume of plays was collected by the author, but he wrote many more which have neither been produced or published.

SIX

The African Image in the Visual Arts

African art, particularly tribal sculpture, influenced the founders of modern European art such as Picasso, Cézanne, Braque, Maurice Vlaminck, Henri Matisse, and others. An appreciation of newly-discovered African art created a vogue among artists and collectors that in turn encouraged African-American artists to use African themes in their work. The black Americans' new pride in their race also contributed to this artistic flowering.

In the United States, painters were spurred on by the Armory Show of 1913 in New York, an exhibition of many of these European modernist artists that provoked much scandal and gained much attention. Through Cubism, African art influenced American artists in the years surrounding World War I as abstract painting gained in popularity.

AARON DOUGLAS

The visual artist most identified with the Harlem Renaissance is painter and muralist Aaron Douglas

Aaron Douglas

(1899–1979). He decorated books by many of the period's leading poets. His explicit use of African-inspired themes makes his work distinctive.

Douglas' featureless figures were usually posed in a landscape suggesting a biblical or mythological story, the images themselves often seeming mysterious. He favored washed-out, cool tones which created a dreamlike world for his tableau. Even in illustrations printed in black and white there is a feeling of unreality. Very few American artists at this time used dreamlike atmospheres this extensively. They are almost surrealist in tone, yet they are never out of place next to the stories and poems with which they are printed.

Among Douglas' most famous work is his set of illustrations for James Weldon Johnson's *God's Trombones*, poems inspired by the sermons of African-American preachers. The paintings represent his best Harlem Renaissance-era style, with their heroic, symbolic figures amidst rainbows, moons, stars, a sprouting tree, the hand of God. These paintings are a modernist retelling of the creation and other biblical stories.

Douglas illustrated some fifteen Harlem Renaissance books and dozens of magazine articles: such works as Alain Locke's *The New Negro*, the 1927 reprint of James Weldon Johnson's classic *The Autobiography of an Ex-Colored Man*, and Claude McKay's three novels, *Home to Harlem, Banjo*, and *Banana Bottom*. Aaron Douglas affirmed the validity of the black experience as a legitimate subject for artists.

HENRY OSSAWA TANNER

In the 1920s the best-known African-American visual artist was the painter Henry Ossawa Tanner (1859–1937). Though he was not a Harlemite, but a Parisian expatriate, his success inspired the younger African-American artists who were struggling to find their own African-American approach to the visual arts.

His last major exhibition, a large solo show of twenty-two paintings, took place in January 1924, at the Grand Central Galleries in Manhattan at the

Henry Ossawa Tanner

height of the Harlem Renaissance. This occasioned
an article on Tanner in the *Crisis* that April, written
by literary editor Jessie Fauset. Virtually all the paintings in that show were either religious scenes or
paintings from his visits to North Africa.

META VAUX WARRICK FULLER

The themes of Paris-educated sculptress Meta Fuller (1877–1968) included African motifs and social protest against racist oppression. Fuller had an exemplary art education at the Pennsylvania Museum School for Industrial Arts, in Paris at the Ecole des Beaux-Arts and the Academie Colarossi, and with sculptor Auguste Rodin at the height of his fame. As a contemporary of Picasso, Fuller also appropriated African motifs.

Her work combines the fierce romanticism from her studies with Rodin with Pan-African-centered concerns, and at least one of her early works anticipated the reworking of African imagery. In 1921, Fuller participated in an exhibition of African-American art at the 135th Street (now known as the Countee Cullen) branch of the New York Public Library.

Fuller's sculptures, such as *Ethiopia Awakening* (1914) and *Mary Turner (A Silent Protest Against Mob Violence)* (1919), directly address issues of concern to African-Americans. Some of her works seem as if they hark back to ancient rituals, while others are expressions of the anguish of African-Americans suffering oppression. She was the first American artist to identify herself with African-centered themes, and she spent part of her life in the world art capital, Paris, just as modernism was discovering Africa.

Many African-American artists who would create distinguished bodies of work in later years first emerged during the Harlem 1920s: painters Palmer Hayden, William H. Johnson, Beauford Delaney, Archibald J. Motley Jr., and Charles Alston; sculptors

Augusta Savage and Richmond Barthe, and photographer James Van Der Zee.

PALMER HAYDEN

Many of these artists were beneficiaries of grants and aid from the Harmon Foundation. Founded by William Harmon, a white millionaire who made his money in real estate, the foundation started an achievement award program for African-American artists and writers in 1926. The first winner was a painter who worked as a janitor at the Foundation offices, Palmer Hayden.

Hayden (1890–1973) is best-known for his paintings of working-class black people in everyday situations. He, like Fuller and Douglas, was also deeply influenced by African art and sought to use imagery he derived from that source in his depictions of his subjects.

Though he was originally thought of as a naive, self-taught painter (a notion which he sometimes encouraged), Hayden did have a considerable formal education. He studied at New York's Cooper Union and at the Boothbay Art Colony in Maine and, after receiving his Harmon fellowship, spent several years in Europe, principally in France. Though criticized for depictions of blacks that exaggerated their features to the point of stereotype, the artist defended himself by claiming he was attempting to develop a style that paid homage to African-American folk traditions. Qualities that come through in his work include a deeply-rooted sense of the absurd and a sharp satirical wit. His most famous paintings include *The Janitor Who Paints* (1939–40), now hanging in the National Museum of American Art in Washington, D.C., and his *John Henry* series, housed in the Museum of African-American Art in Los Angeles.

ARCHIBALD J. MOTLEY JR.

Archibald J. Motley Jr. (1891–1980) had his first solo show in New York in 1928, at the New Gallery on Madison Avenue. The show was such an artistic and commercial success that it was the cause of a front page feature article in *The New York Times.*

The twenty-six paintings exhibited in that two-week show included nightclub and dance scenes and genre scenes. His most famous paintings of this period capture the rhythm and style of jazz-age life, using iridescent colors and figures with sharply defined features. He, too, used humor in setting up his scenes, and sometimes edges toward caricature.

In struggling with how to use African art in their work, Harlem Renaissance artists were trying to use images that had been seen before only as racist stereotypes. They sought to reclaim those stereotypes in a way that escaped caricature. Often they did not succeed. But Motley left a great body of work that documents a pioneering artist, striving to build an African-American artistic tradition. A retrospective of his work was held in 1992 at the Studio Museum in Harlem.

WILLIAM H. JOHNSON

William H. Johnson (1901–1970) was an extremely talented painter whose work only became widely appreciated several decades after his death. He lived in Harlem and studied with Charles Webster Hawthorne at the School of the National Academy of Design in New York and at Hawthorne's Cape Cod School of Art in Provincetown, Massachusetts, for five years. Johnson moved to Paris in 1926 and, except for a six-month stay in the United States in 1929 to 1930, lived abroad for the next decade.

While living in New York Johnson won a Harmon Foundation Gold Medal. Johnson's late-1920s style was influenced by expressionist painters then the rage in Paris such as Chaim Soutine (1894–1943). He had several solo shows in Europe, and was acquainted with other African-American expatriate artists, including Henry Ossawa Tanner.

CARL VAN VECHTEN

Novelist, journalist, and photographer, Carl Van Vechten captured many Harlem Renaissance celebrities in a series of astonishing portraits. In his photos, nearly always taken in a studio setting, Van Vechten strove to bring out the emotional character he saw projected by the artist. Therefore, we get a portrait of Bessie Smith in which the great blues singer is a conveyor of pathos and sadness, or a proud, almost stern James Weldon Johnson. Van Vechten's excellent photos stand as beautiful monuments to the men and women who created the Harlem Renaissance. Indeed, an entire history of the 1920s artistic movement in Harlem can be written simply be describing the body of work Van Vechten built during those years.

JAMES VAN DER ZEE

Those who want to get a visual glimpse of the real-life Harlem—its celebrities as well as its working people—need go no further than the photographs of James Van Der Zee (1886–1983). From the photographic studio he set up on Harlem's 135th Street in 1917, Van Der Zee set about taking literally hun-

A James Van Der Zee photo of children receiving food bags from nuns in 1932

dreds of pictures. His subjects were the neighborhood's residents. Some of those residents, of course, were famous. Van Der Zee's subjects included Bessie Smith, Florence Mills, Countee Cullen, Jack Johnson, and dozens of others. He was also the photographer of choice for family and individual portraits, weddings, funerals, social and civic clubs, and grand events, and the official photographer for Marcus Garvey's Universal Negro Improvement Association. Most of Van Der Zee's work has never been seen, and exists in private collections.

His art captured, as no photographer had done previously, the elegance and beauty of black people. Since African-Americans were his customers, Van Der Zee strove to capture the African image in photography in a way that would please the photographic subjects. Dark skin tones in Van Der Zee's eyes, then, become a compositional element in a conscious way, with no hint of exoticism.

The African-American visual artists broke new ground primarily by making genuine, nondemonized representations of African people. They also began to make themselves known, not just as isolated individuals, but as a group of black artists who were creating an enduring body of work.

The limited fraternity between African-American painters and sculptors and their white colleagues probably had a negative effect on American art. It certainly led to a situation that has kept black American artists from being acknowledged. Nevertheless, in the United States at least, the full and free absorption of the African image in art, a cornerstone of European-influenced modernist art, was first embarked upon by black artists whose careers (with the exception of Meta Vaux Warrick Fuller) started during the Harlem Renaissance.

SEVEN

The Renaissance Abroad

Josephine Baker was the first black American international entertainment superstar and the first African-American actress to play starring roles with dignity in motion pictures. She was also the first to affirm, for an international public, the beauty of black skin and of African form and culture on the stage. She transformed what was called a "savage" (African) dance into a performance of compelling sensual beauty. She was an early exponent of the Harlem Renaissance ideas about the beauty of African images and people. Such beauty made her a star. She did all this as a resident of France for the fifty years following her arrival in 1925. By the time she arrived in Paris, she was already a veteran of the theatrical stage, having danced in several shows, the most famous of which was *Shuffle Along*.

Baker came to Paris with one of the innumerable African-American stage shows that had been touring Europe for decades. Since the end of World War I, the number of black American artists who went

Josephine Baker

abroad to live had begun to rise. And why not? Like their white counterparts, the blacks found Europe, and especially Paris, a cheap, friendly place to live. The exchange rate, in the winter of 1925 to 1926, was one dollar for twenty-five francs. The year before, four dollars had bought Langston Hughes the cheapest hotel room in the Paris neighborhood of Montmartre for two weeks.

Malcolm Cowley, in *Exile's Return*, wrote of the Paris of the mid-1920s and the Americans who flocked there: "They came to recover the good life and the traditions of art, to free themselves from organized stupidity, to win their deserved place in the hierarchy of the intellect." For the black artists, the "organized stupidity" took the form of organized (and unorganized) racism.[1]

The city was so popular with Americans that George Gershwin, a composer who learned his craft on Tin Pan Alley (from, among others, his good friend the African-American arranger Will Vodery), created a tribute to it. In 1924 *An American In Paris* premiered in New York. He played it with the Paul Whiteman orchestra. Whiteman led an enormously popular dance band and was billed the King of Jazz during the 1920s. This white disciple of the black New York syncopated orchestra music used only white musicians, even though one of the great arrangers for those orchestras, composer William Grant Still, wrote some of Whiteman's arrangements.

By October 1925, when Josephine Baker opened in *La Revue Negre* at the Theatre des Champs-Elysees (she started playing the Folies Bergere the following March), there were forty-three thousand Americans in Paris.

The headliner of *La Revue Negre* was the nineteen-year-old, exquisitely beautiful Josephine Baker. Baker was a sensation. The show she starred in was the typical mix of vaudeville routines like those she had performed in *Shuffle Along, Chocolate Dandies*, and *In Bamville*, the Sissle and Blake revues produced in

New York. The show had plantation scenes and skits of blacks newly arrived in the city.

The band, led by pianist Claude Hopkins, was notable, in part, because it had saxophonist and clarinetist Sidney Bechet, one of the great master New Orleans jazz musicians, as a member. Bechet played a solo number on stage that helped enhance his legend. Bechet would eventually settle in Europe, living much of the rest of his life—except for the World War II years—in France, where he died, in 1959, a rich and famous man.

La Revue Negre made Baker a star. She went on to make several films and had an outstanding recording career. By the time she died in 1975, she had recorded 230 songs. She became a heroine of the French Resistance against the Nazis in World War II, and made France her permanent home.

Langston Hughes remembered in *The Big Sea* the reaction of the first black Americans he encountered on arriving in Paris in the spring of 1924. He told them he was looking for work.

"They scowled at me. Finally one of them said: 'Well, what instrument do you play?'" Hughes replied, after some more questioning of this sort, that no, he wasn't a musician, didn't tap dance, but was just looking for a job. "Any kind of job."[2]

They thought he was crazy. "There ain't no 'any kind of job' here." There were plenty of French people looking for work. If you can't sing or dance, they told him, then he might as well go home.[3]

He did find a job, in a Montmartre cabaret. A few weeks later, the club, Le Grand Duc, welcomed a new blues singer, Ada Smith, from the United States. It was a small place, just twelve tables, with a bar not big enough for six pair of elbows. Smith, whose stage name was Bricktop (for her shocking red hair), told the manager, Gene Bullard, "My, this a nice little bar. Now where's the cabaret?" "This is it," he told her. She burst into tears. A waiter came to her aid, fed her, and calmed her down. Years later, Bricktop wrote, "I didn't know, the waiters didn't know, nobody knew who he was." Hughes wasn't famous. Bricktop was better known, having performed in vaudeville and as a star at such fancy Harlem clubs as Barron Wilkins' Exclusive Club and at Connie's Inn.[4]

Most of the black Americans in Paris were musicians who had brought to Paris the ragtime-based, syncopated dance-music style jazz that was played in most northern American cities before New Orleans and other southern musicians arrived in big numbers in the early 1920s. Many of these musicians were veterans of James Reese Europe's 369th U.S. Infantry Band (also known as the "Hellfighters") who had stayed in or returned to France and other European countries after the armistice.

Jazz musicians had been visiting Europe since jazz began. And, before that, minstrel shows toured European capitals. But in the 1920s, jazz really grew in popularity. These bands played clubs all over Europe, and some of them made their home in Paris. It was in Paris, in fact, that Langston Hughes met the legendary drummer Buddy Gilmore, who played after-hours sessions at Le Grand Duc, where Hughes was working. "The cream of the Negro musicians then in France" played Le Grand Duc, Hughes wrote in *The Big Sea*. He was talking about people like trumpeter Cricket Smith, violinist Louis Jones, pianist Palmer Jones (husband of Florence Embry), clarinetist Frank Withers, and Buddy Gilmore. These musicians "would weave music that would almost make your heart stand still at dawn in a Paris night club in the Rue Pigalle." Hughes listened while finishing his shift at the club, washing dishes in a two feet by four feet kitchen, "with the fire in the range dying and the one high window letting the soft light in."[5]

The experience of those nights—actually early mornings—would serve as inspiration for some of Hughes' finest jazz poetry, especially the famous "Jazz Band in a Parisian Cabaret," which first appeared in the *Crisis* of December 1925, and then in his second book, *Fine Clothes to the Jew* (1927).

The experience abroad of the most successful Harlem Renaissance artists set a pattern that was repeated after World War II. For many black artists, success in Europe would be achieved in the wake of the Great Depression. This is particularly true of musicians such as Louis Armstrong and Duke Ellington, both of whom traveled to Europe for the first time during the early 1930s. These tours made them world famous.

Langston Hughes also became internationally famous during the 1930s. The political climate of the period, marked first and foremost by the rise of fascism and the international resistance to it led by the left-wing movement was an influence under which Hughes made his reputation. He would become one of the most famous left-wing poets in the world and probably the world's most famous American poet. Certainly he was so for people of African descent. His books were translated into Chinese and Russian and his fame in those countries far exceeded his considerable notoriety in the country of his birth.

Today the African-American colony in Paris is filled with writers, actors, and, especially, musicians. Some of the famous post-World War II African-American artists who have lived in France include novelists Richard Wright, William Gardner Smith, and Chester Himes; poet Ted Joans; and many, many jazz and popular musicians. They go there because they're looking for the same things that propelled artists in the 1920s to leave home for this most nurturing of artistic capitals.

EIGHT

Free Within Ourselves

Between the stock market crash of October 24, 1929, and the Harlem riots of March 19 and 20, 1935, the artistic movement that existed in Harlem disappeared. Some of the major figures of the Harlem Renaissance died young. Novelists Wallace Thurman and Rudolph Fisher died during the same week in December 1934. Some of the better known 1920s musicians, like Bubber Miley, Joseph King Oliver, and Bessie Smith, also died in the 1930s. But many others, including Cab Calloway (who replaced Ellington at the Cotton Club), Chick Webb, Fletcher Henderson, and especially Duke Ellington would do very well in the thirties, the great era of the jazz orchestra.

For some time in the early 1930s it seemed like nothing had changed. Many of the nightspots and the theaters were as crowded as they had been during the twenties. People still danced all night at places like the Savoy Ballroom and the Rockland Palace. The Cotton Club, Connie's Inn, and Small's were still open, as were innumerable speakeasies and small clubs throughout the community. The Apollo Theater opened in 1934 and became a main showcase for African-American performing artists. The Savoy Ballroom, Harlem's largest, was jumping, as it would continue to do for many years to come. But as the 1930s wore on, a new center of the city's nightclub life emerged further downtown, away from the African-American community, out of increasingly ghettoized Harlem.

Many of the artistic luminaries were less and less visible in the old neighborhood. Some, like Langston Hughes, Louis Armstrong, or Duke Ellington, spent much of the early 1930s traveling or living abroad or elsewhere in the United States. Others, like James Weldon Johnson and Aaron Douglas, found jobs teaching in universities. As for the Harlem they left behind, the neighborhood itself was, despite its gaiety and continuing vibrant community life, increasingly mired in the Great Depression.

The nationwide economic catastrophe known as the Great Depression was especially hard on Harlem. Behind the nightlife, parties, and the literary and artistic community lived a community that composed "the poorest, the unhealthiest, the unhappiest and the most crowded single large section of New York City," a reporter wrote in the February 10, 1930 *New York Herald Tribune.*

In the quarter-century since real-estate developer Philip Payton brought African-Americans to this once affluent suburb, the black population had grown by 600 percent. Half of the population lived on unemployment relief in 1930. Combined with the dismal wages of those lucky enough to have jobs and the presence of streams of new migrants from the South (who were leaving conditions even worse than those found in Harlem), conditions deteriorated daily. People were so poor that as many as twenty evictions a day took place in Harlem in 1931.

"All of Harlem is pervaded by a sense of congestion," commented novelist James Baldwin, who was a six-year-old neighborhood boy in 1930. Writing many years later in *Notes of a Native Son*, he compared life in the emerging ghetto to "the insistent, maddening, claustrophobic pounding in the skull that comes from trying to breathe in a very small room with all the windows shut."[1]

In 1926, the year *The Weary Blues* appeared, Langston Hughes wrote in an essay "The Negro Artist and the Racial Mountain" in *The Nation* magazine about "the mountain standing in the way of any true Negro art in America." The mountain was "this urge within the race toward whiteness, the desire to pour racial individuality into the mold of American standardization."[2]

The essay was a kind of manifesto of the Harlem Renaissance. "For the American Negro artist," Hughes wrote, there is "a great field of unused material ready for his own art." African-American life, he wrote, provides "sufficient matter to furnish a black artist with a lifetime of creative work." But first that artist must overcome the "racial" mountain.

The mountain Hughes spoke about was the racial self-loathing he found, especially among middle-class and "high-class" African-Americans. In such environments, Hughes wrote "the word white comes to be unconsciously a symbol of all the virtues."

Arguing for an art that willingly draws inspiration from African-American culture, Hughes said "most of my own poems are racial in theme and treatment." Their subject matter is a sincere reflection of his life as a black American. "And yet after every reading I answer questions like these from my own people: Do you think Negroes should always write about Negroes? I wish you wouldn't read some of your poems to white folks. How do you find anything interesting in a place like a cabaret? Why do you write about black people?"

The message here, Hughes said, is that his questioners believe black culture is something to be ashamed of. He accuses his questioners of secretly wanting to be white. The duty of the black artist, he said, is "to change through the force of his art that old whispering 'I want to be white,' hidden in the aspiration of his people, to 'Why should I want to be white? I am a Negro—and beautiful!'"

"The Negro Artist and the Racial Mountain" closes with a ringing call for the black artist to embrace the sights and sounds of black culture as material for art. "We younger Negro artists who create now intend to express our individual dark-skinned selves without fear or shame," Hughes wrote. "If colored people are pleased we are glad. If they are not, their displeasure doesn't matter either. We build our temples for tomorrow, strong as we know how, and we stand on top of the mountain, free within ourselves."

This sentiment is what the Harlem Renaissance was all about. For the first time, an artistic and cultural movement emerged in which black artists, musicians, and writers began to celebrate themselves and their culture. The Harlem Renaissance marked the rise of the self-aware African-American artistic voice to match the long developing African-American political voice, which itself reached a new maturity in the 1920s, a voice that would indelibly mark twentieth century world culture. The mask Paul Laurence Dunbar wrote about—"it hides our cheeks and shades our eyes"—was no longer the only public face black people showed the world.

SOURCE NOTES

CHAPTER ONE

1. Booker T. Washington, *Up From Slavery* (New York: Viking Penguin, 1986), 126, 218–225.

2. Edmund David Cronin, *Black Moses: The Story of Marcus Garvey and the Universal Negro Improvement Association* (Madison: University of Wisconsin, 1955), 65.

3. Paul Laurence Dunbar, *Lyrics of the Lowly Life* (New York: Citadel, 1984), 167, 195.

4. "Sympathy" is in Countee Cullen's *Caroling Dusk: An Anthology of Verse by Black Poets of the Twenties* (New York: Citadel, 1993), 8–9.

CHAPTER TWO

1. Claude McKay, *Selected Poems of Claude McKay* (New York: Harcourt Brace Jovanovich, 1953), 36.

2. Countee Cullen, *My Soul's High Song: The Collected Writings of Countee Cullen*, Gerald Early, ed. (New York: Anchor Doubleday, 1991).

3. Arnold Rampersad and David Roessel, *The Collected Poems of Langston Hughes* (New York: Alfred A. Knopf, 1994), 50.

4. James Weldon Johnson, *God's Trombones: Seven Negro Sermons in Verse* (New York: The Viking Press, 1927), 17–20.

5. Sterling Brown, *The Collected Poems of Sterling Brown*, Michael S. Harper, ed. (New York: Harper, 1979), 62.

6. For Fenton Johnson, see James Weldon Johnson, ed., *The Book of American Negro Poetry*, 140–146; Countee Cullen, ed., *Caroling Dusk* (New York: Citadel, 1993), 61–64; and Arna Bontemps, ed., *American Negro Poetry* (New York: Hill and Wang, 1963), 25–28.

7. Maureen Honey, ed., *Shadowed Dreams: Women's Poetry of the Harlem Renaissance* (New Brunswick: Rutgers, 1989).

CHAPTER THREE

1. Duke Ellington, *Music is My Mistress* (New York: Da Capo, 1980), 106.

2. Ibid., 107.

3. Willie "The Lion" Smith and George Hoefer, *Music On My Mind* (New York: Da Capo, 1978), 100–105.

4. Philip Horton, *Hart Crane: The Life of an American Poet* (New York: Viking, 1957), 123.

CHAPTER FOUR

1. Quoted in Robert Hemenway, ed., *The Black Novelist* (Columbus: Charles E. Merrill, 1970), 148–149.

2. Ibid., 149.

CHAPTER SEVEN

1. Malcolm Cowley, *Exile's Return* (New York: Viking/ Compass, 1956), 81.

2. Langston Hughes, *The Big Sea* (New York: Hill and Wang, 1963), 229.

3. Ibid., 150

CHAPTER EIGHT

1. James Baldwin, *Notes of a Native Son* (New York: Dial, 1963), 51.

2. Quoted in Addison Gayle, ed., *The Black Aesthetic* (New York: Viking, 1972), 167–172.

BIBLIOGRAPHY

Albertson, Chris. *Bessie*. New York: Stein and Day, 1974.

Anderson, Jervis. *This Was Harlem*. New York: Farrar Straus & Giroux, 1982.

Baker, Houston A., Jr., *Modernism and the Harlem Renaissance*. Chicago: University of Chicago Press, 1987.

Baldwin, James. *Notes of a Native Son*. New York: Dial, 1963.

Batchelor, Denzil. *Jack Johnson and His Times*. London: George Weidenfeld & Nicholson, 1990.

Bontemps, Arna. *American Negro Poetry*. New York: Hill and Wang, 1963.

———. *The Harlem Renaissance Remembered*. New York: Dodd, Mead & Company, 1972.

Bontemps, Arna, and Langston Hughes. *Letters, 1925–67*. New York: Paragon, 1990.

Braithwaite, William Stanley. "The Negro in American Literature," in Locke, *The New Negro.* W. S. Braithwaite, Philip Butcher, ed., *The William Stanley Braithwaite Reader.* Ann Arbor: University of Michigan, 1972.

Brown, Sterling A. *The Collected Poems of Sterling A. Brown,* Michael S. Harper, ed. New York: Harper, 1979.

Charters and Kunstadt. *Jazz, a History of the New York Scene.* New York: Doubleday 1962; New York: Da Capo, 1981.

Chestnutt, Charles W. *The Wife of His Youth and other Stories.* Boston and New York: Houghton Mifflin, 1899; Ann Arbor: University of Michigan, 1977.

Chilton, John. *Who's Who in Jazz.* New York: Time-Life, 1978.

Collier, James Lincoln. *Duke Ellington.* New York: Oxford University Press, 1987.

Cooper, Wayne F. *Claude McKay: Rebel Sojourner in the Harlem Renaissance.* Baton Rouge: Louisiana State University, 1987; New York: Schocken, 1990.

Cowley, Malcolm. *Exile's Return.* New York: Viking/Compass, 1956.

Cronin, Edmund David. *Black Moses: The Story of Marcus Garvey and the Universal Negro Improvement Association.* Madison: University of Wisconsin, 1955.

Cullen, Countee. *My Soul's High Song: The Collected Writings of Countee Cullen,* Gerald Early, ed. New York: Anchor Doubleday, 1991.

Cullen, Countee, ed. *Caroling Dusk: An Anthology of Verse by Black Poets of the Twenties*. New York: Harper and Brothers, 1927; New York: Citadel, 1993.

Duberman, Martin Bauml. *Paul Robeson*. New York: Alfred A. Knopf, 1988.

Duconge', Ada Smith, with James Haskins. *Bricktop*. New York: Antheneum, 1983.

Dunbar, Paul Laurence. *Lyrics of the Lowly Life*. New York: Citadel, 1984.

———. *The Sport of the Gods*. New York: Dodd, Mead & Company, 1981.

Ellington, Duke. *Music Is My Mistress*. New York: Da Capo, 1980.

Finch, Noel Riley. *Sylvia Beach and the Lost Generation*. New York: Norton, 1983.

Fitzgerald, F. Scott. *The Great Gatsby*. New York: Scribner, 1925.

Five Plays by Langston Hughes. Bloomington: Indiana University Press, 1968.

Foner, Eric. *Reconstruction: America's Unfinished Revolution, 1863–1877*. New York: Harper and Row, 1988.

Gates, Henry Louis, Jr., ed. *Classic Slave Narratives*. New York: Mentor, 1987.

Giddings, Paula: *When and Where I Enter: The Impact of Black Women on Race and Sex in America*. New York: Bantam, 1985.

Giddins, Gary. *Satchmo*. New York: Doubleday, 1988.

Glaysher, Frederick, ed. *Robert Hayden: Collected Poems.* New York: Liveright, 1985.

Goddard, Chris. *Jazz Away from Home.* New York, London: Paddington Press, 1979.

Golding, John. *Cubism,* 3rd ed. Cambridge: Harvard University Press, 1988.

Goldwater, Robert. *Primitivism in Modern Art.* New York: Vintage, 1967.

Gregory, H., and M. Zaturenska. *A History of American Poetry: 1900–1940.* New York: Harcourt Brace, 1946.

Haskins, Jim. *The Cotton Club.* New York: Plume, 1977.

Hemenway, Robert, ed. *The Black Novelist.* Columbus: Charles E. Merrill, 1970.

Hemenway, Robert. *Zora Neale Hurston: A Literary Biography.* Urbana and Chicago: University of Illinois, 1980.

Hentoff, Nat. "Jazz in the Twenties: Garvin Bushell," in Williams, Martin, ed., *Jazz Panorama.* New York: Collier, 1964.

Honey, Maureen, ed. *Shadowed Dreams: Women's Poetry of the Harlem Renaissance.* New Brunswick: Rutgers University Press, 1989.

Horton, Philip. *Hart Crane: The Life of an American Poet.* New York: Viking, 1957.

Hughes, Langston. *The Big Sea.* New York: Hill and Wang, 1963.

Jabes, Edmond. *The Book of Questions,* translated by Rosemarie Waldrop. New York: Wesleyan, 1984.

Johnson, James Weldon. *Along This Way*. New York: Viking Penguin, 1933; New York: Penguin, 1990.

————. *Autobiography of an Ex-Coloured Man*. New York: Alfred A. Knopf, 1927; New York: Hill and Wang, 1960.

————. *Black Manhattan*. New York, 1930; New York: Atheneum, 1968.

————. *The Book of American Negro Poetry*. New York: Harcourt Brace & World, 1922, 1931, 1959.

————. *God's Trombones: Seven Negro Sermons in Verse*. New York: The Viking Press, 1927.

Karl, Frederick R. *Modern and Modernism: The Sovereignty of the Artist, 1885–1925*. New York: Atheneum, 1985.

Kimball, Robert. Record liner notes for *Shuffle Along*. New York: New World Records (NW260), 1976.

Kirkeby, Ed. *Ain't Misbehavin'*. New York: Dodd, Mead & Company, 1966.

Larsen, Nella. *Quicksand*. New York: Alfred A. Knopf, 1928. *Passing*, New York: Alfred A. Knopf, 1929. *Quicksand and Passing*, New Brunswick: Rutgers, 1994.

Lewis, David Levering. *When Harlem Was in Vogue*. New York: Oxford University Press, 1989.

————. *W. E. B. Du Bois: Biography of a Race*. New York: Henry Holt, 1993.

Locke, Alain. *The New Negro*. New York: Albert & Charles Boni, 1925; New York: Atheneum, 1968.

Martin, Tony. *Literary Garveyism: Garvey, Black Arts and the Harlem Renaissance.* Dover: The Majority Press, 1983.

Maryemma, Graham. "Frances Ellen Watkins Harper," in *Dictionary of Literary Biography,* vol. 50. Detroit: Free Press, 1986

McKay, Claude. *A Long Way from Home.* New York: Harcourt Brace Jovanovich, 1970.

———. *Home to Harlem.* New York: Harper, 1928, 1965.

———. *Selected Poems of Claude McKay.* New York: Harcourt Brace Jovanovich, 1953.

Melba, Joyce Boyd. *Discarded Legacy: Politics and Poetics in the Life of Frances E.W. Harper, 1825–1911.* Detroit: Wayne State University Press, 1994.

Mosby, Dewey F., et al. *Henry Ossawa Tanner.* Philadelphia: Philadelphia Museum of Art, 1991.

Murray, Peter and Linda. *A Dictionary of Art and Artists.* Baltimore: Penguin, 1963.

Norman, Charles. *Poets and People.* New York: Bobbs-Merrill, 1972. Norman also wrote *Ezra Pound* (New York: Minerva, 1969).

Osofsky, Gilbert. *Harlem: The Making of a Ghetto.* New York: Harper & Row, 1971.

Rampersad, Arnold. *The Life of Langston Hughes,* vol. 1: *I, Too, Sing America.* New York: Oxford University Press, 1986.

Rampersad, Arnold, and David Roessel. *The Collected Poems of Langston Hughes.* New York: Alfred A. Knopf, 1994.

Rexroth, Kenneth. *American Poetry in the Twentieth Century.* New York: Herder and Herder, 1971.

Rose, Al. *Eubie Blake.* New York: Schirmer, 1979.

Rothenberg, Jerome, ed. *Revolution of the Word.* New York: Seabury, 1974.

Scheaffer, Louis. *O'Neill: Son and Artist.* New York: Paragon, 1990.

Schoener, Allon. *Harlem on My Mind.* New York: Random House, 1968.

Smith, Willie "The Lion," and George Hoefer. *Music on My Mind.* New York: Da Capo, 1978.

Smith, Cecil. *The Musical Comedy in America.* New York: Theatre Arts Books, 1950.

Studio Museum in Harlem. *Harlem Renaissance: Art in Black America.* New York: Harry N. Abrams, 1987.

Robinson, Dr. Jontyle Theresa. "Archibald John Motley, Jr.: A Notable Anniversary for a Pioneer," in *Three Masters: Eldzier Cortor, Hughie Lee-Smith, Archibald John Motley, Jr.* New York: Kenkeleba Gallery, 1988.

Thurman, Wallace. *The Blacker the Berry.* New York: Macaulay, 1929; New York: Macmillan, 1970.

Toomer, Jean. *Cane.* New York: Boni & Liveright, 1923; New York: Liveright, 1975.

Torrence, Ridgely. *The Story of John Hope.* New York: Macmillan, 1948.

Tuttle, William M., Jr. *Race Riot: Chicago in the Red Summer of 1919.* New York: Atheneum, 1972.

Ulanov, Barry. *A History of Jazz in America*. New York: Viking, 1952.

Untermeyer, Louis, ed. *Modern American Poetry*, 3rd rev. ed. New York: Harcourt, Brace and Company, 1925.

Vincent, Theodore G. *Black Power and the Garvey Movement*. San Francisco: Ramparts Press, 1972.

Washington, Booker T. *Up From Slavery*. New York: Doubleday, Page & Co., 1901; New York: Viking Penguin, 1986.

Weber, Brom, ed. *The Complete Poems and Selected Letters and Prose of Hart Crane*. New York: Liveright, 1966; New York: Anchor, 1966.

Williams, William Carlos. "Spring and All," in *Collected Poems*, vol. 1. New York: New Directions, 1986.

INDEX